D1082157

Managing Social Media in Libraries

CHANDOS
SOCIAL MEDIA SERIES

Series Editors: Geoff Walton and Woody Evans
(emails: g.l.walton@staffs.ac.uk and kdevans@gmail.com)

This series of books is aimed at practitioners and academics involved in using social media in all its forms and in any context. This includes information professionals, academics, librarians and managers, and leaders in business. Social media can enhance services, build communication channels, and create competitive advantage. The impact of these new media and decisions that surround their use in business can no longer be ignored. The delivery of education, privacy issues, logistics, political activism and research rounds out the series' coverage. As a resource to complement the understanding of issues relating to other areas of information science, teaching and related areas, books in this series respond with practical applications. If you would like a full listing of current and forthcoming titles, please visit our website www.chandospublishing.com or email wp@woodheadpublishing.com or telephone +44 (0) 1223 499140.

New authors: we are always pleased to receive ideas for new titles; if you would like to write a book for Chandos in the area of social media, please contact Jonathan Davis, Commissioning Editor, on jonathan.davis@chandospublishing.com or telephone +44 (0) 1993 848726.

Bulk orders: some organisations buy a number of copies of our books. If you are interested in doing this, we would be pleased to discuss a discount. Please email wp@woodheadpublishing.com or telephone +44 (0) 1223 499140.

Managing Social Media in Libraries

Finding collaboration, coordination, and focus

TROY A. SWANSON

Oxford Cambridge New Delhi

ascma

WISSER MEMORIAL LIBRARY

Z674.75
.S63
S93
2012
c.1

Chandos Publishing
Hexagon House
Avenue 4
Station Lane
Witney
Oxford OX28 4BN
UK
Tel: +44 (0) 1993 848726
E-mail: info@chandospublishing.com
www.chandospublishing.com
www.chandospublishingonline.com

Chandos Publishing is an imprint of Woodhead Publishing Limited

Woodhead Publishing Limited
80 High Street
Sawston
Cambridge CB22 3HJ
UK
Tel: +44 (0) 1223 499140
Fax: +44 (0) 1223 832819
www.woodheadpublishing.com

First published in 2012

ISBN: 978-1-84334-711-8 (print)
ISBN: 978-1-78063-377-0 (online)

Chandos Social Media Series ISSN: 2050-6813 (print) and ISSN: 2050-6821 (online)

© T. A. Swanson, 2012

British Library Cataloguing-in-Publication Data.
A catalogue record for this book is available from the British Library.

All rights reserved. No part of this publication may be reproduced, stored in or introduced into a retrieval system, or transmitted, in any form, or by any means (electronic, mechanical, photocopying, recording or otherwise) without the prior written permission of the publisher. This publication may not be lent, resold, hired out or otherwise disposed of by way of trade in any form of binding or cover other than that in which it is published without the prior consent of the publisher. Any person who does any unauthorised act in relation to this publication may be liable to criminal prosecution and civil claims for damages.

The publisher makes no representation, express or implies, with regard to the accuracy of the information contained in this publication and cannot accept any legal responsibility or liability for any errors or omissions.

The material contained in this publication constitutes general guidelines only and does not represent to be advice on any particular matter. No reader or purchaser should act on the basis of material contained in this publication without first taking professional advice appropriate to their particular circumstances. All screenshots in this publication are the copyright of the website owner(s), unless indicated otherwise.

Typeset by Domex e-Data Pvt. Ltd., India
Printed in the UK and USA.

Contents

List of figures

List of abbreviations

DOS	disk operating system
GPS	global positioning system
HTML	hypertext markup language
ILS	integrated library system
IT	information technology
MARC	machine readable cataloging
MP3	MPEG Audio Layer III
OPAC	online public access catalog
PDF	Portable Document Format
PR	public relations
RSS	RDF Site Summary or Really Simple Syndication
VoIP	Voice over Internet Protocol
WYSIWYG	what you see is what you get
XML	Extensible Markup Language

Acknowledgements

As with anything in life, nothing is a solo endeavor, and this book is no different, so I must acknowledge and thank all the people who made this work possible.

First, I must start with my family. Thanks to Kim, Skylar, Parker and Lainey. During a stressful year when we welcomed Lainey into our lives, you put up with me working on this book. Your support made this possible.

I want to send a very special thank you to the people who read my manuscript as it was in process. I especially want to thank Marea Kahn who read the first drafts of each chapter and gave me very valuable input and direction. Your input was instrumental in shaping this text.

Back in 2003, I had never heard of a blog until Jenny Levine (*@shifted*) introduced me to them. Then she hosted our first blogs for us. The very talented Larry Sloma led our implementation, and Michael Stephens showed us how blogs can connect people. Jenny, Michael and Larry helped our library move into social media before we understood it. Thanks!

I want to thank Carolyn, Vandella, Larry, Emily, Lori and Julie, all of whom were in my cohort from the 2004 SYNERGY: The Illinois Library Leadership Initiative. They helped me to understand my career path and ultimately to recommit to community college libraries. This led to my PhD and some of the foundational research that became this book. Professional and personal development is a team sport, and I have had a great team.

Finally, thanks to all of you who believe that libraries are more than books, articles and quiet spaces. We know that libraries are powerful and transformative organizations. Our challenge is to demonstrate our value and change our world. It is my hope that this text is a small step in the right direction.

Foreword

Communications technology continues to connect and change the world. This can be desired and leveraged in many useful ways. Libraries using the web have evolved from static informational and contact style pages to more dynamic and interactive sites. It could be argued that social media have been one of the greatest advancements in this evolution. For the last decade, we have debated, explored and implemented various social tools. I am lucky to have written and spoken about these topics around the world.

I have also been lucky to engage with some very smart and forward-thinking individuals, including Jenny Levine, the Shifted Librarian; Michael Casey, originator of the Library 2.0 service philosophy; and Troy Swanson who managed the Moraine Valley Library's social media and website. I met Troy at Internet Librarian 2006, and we had an intense and enlightening discussion about tying emerging technological tools to mission statements and the goals of the institution.

Consider the following statements related to Moraine Valley Library's use of podcasts which I posted on Tame the Web back in 2006:

- They fulfill the library's mission by "providing information literacy instruction and support across the curriculum" and "collaborating with faculty and others to develop innovative services and programs."

- They enhance the classroom experience by providing expert views on challenging and timely subjects.

- They provide an opportunity for students and community members to participate in library events even though they may not be able to visit the events in person.

I appreciate the emphasis on moving away from place-based thinking about library programs and services. Offering access to events via a recording, shared and disseminated via podcast feeds and present on the library blog may seem quaint now, but this foundational practice paved the way for many other innovations with Web 2.0.

The book you are holding is a reflection and critical analysis of the use of social media in libraries that rises above and beyond the typical tool-of-the-month style tomes and provides something much more important: a detailed analysis of the whys of social media and the hows of getting staff and library users involved. The viewpoints shared here by Troy align with my own research as well. My dissertation focused on early librarian bloggers and the sense of community they found within the burgeoning blogosphere. Connecting, sharing and finding a clear path through a new landscape of social connections were definitely part of the pragmatic biblioblogger's experience. Recently, my examination of library staff use of social tools as part of Learning 2.0 programs in Australia further supports the idea that with experience and exploration comes confidence and willingness to participate in the greater community.

Let the technology fall away and what is left is a guide to facilitating and encouraging conversations—a way to tell a story. "Storytelling is a powerful tool," Troy writes, "and social media represent a way to extend our own stories." Moving the story beyond the physical *place* of the library so it exists online to be accessed and enhanced with multiple voices should be the goal of every information organization.

Troy has synthesized and collected his own ongoing critical thinking and extensive experience with this work.

Troy explores a number of questions: how should one involve staff in sharing the library's story? Should individual librarians connect with individual users? How can social media guidelines guide the use of the tools in an evolving and unrestricted manner?

He also addresses the challenges that occur as libraries shift some focus to emerging technologies. Many of these challenges are people-focused, rather than issues with the technologies themselves. "The challenge around effective social media implementation is to get library staff to see social media as an integral part of their jobs so that they choose to participate." This challenge can be solved with transparency and a clearly defined, yet evolving mission: "If people are fearful of participation or do not see the value of participation, they will not participate."

Troy writes, "Libraries that have not dabbled in social media may wonder where they should start. The answer may sound straight out of 2004, but it remains true: start a good blog. Blogs remain the most flexible social media tool." I've written extensively about blogging and published my own research on the perceptions and experience of the LIS blogger. I wholeheartedly agree that the blog as platform can be a powerful content management system for telling your library's story. Combine that tool and the others explored in this work with Dr Swanson's insights and critically-focused big-picture thinking, and you have a solid path toward engaging your community and encouraging the heart of the user.

Michael Stephens
Assistant Professor, School of Library & Information Science, San Jose State University and creator of the award-winning Tame The Web blog

Preface: make social media fit your library

Introduction

When I talk to people about social media, I am often asked an underhanded question. The question goes something like, "do you have any evidence for the number of people who use social media in libraries?" I have been asked this by researchers at conferences, reviewers of several of my manuscripts, and IT managers at my own campus. They say it with a touch of disdain. What they mean to say is, "no one reads blogs or cares about blogs." They see Facebook as a place where high-school kids post concert photos. To them, social media are not serious.

Yet, if you read the library literature or attend library conferences, social media have at times been held up as the savior of libraries. Some authors make it sound like blogs were invented for libraries and that libraries were invented to blog. Don't worry about circulating books or the number of transactions at the reference desk, we have Facebook. Sometimes it sounds as if there is no problem that librarians can't tweet away.

The reality is somewhere in the middle. Social media can definitely help librarians reach out and make connections. Still, practicing librarians should be concerned at how little traffic our social media sites see. I have interviewed blog authors who sheepishly admit that they long for more interaction from readers. They would even welcome negative comments that were not spam. In a survey for *D-Lib Magazine*, Michalis Gerolimos (2011) found that college library Facebook pages had a relatively small number of people following the page; furthermore, interaction was almost entirely limited to staff members.

Despite this finding, I am not sure how libraries can afford *not* to use social media. The world is changing around us, and we are doing our best to keep up. I think that libraries should keep in mind the demise of the video rental business.

Not too long ago, the video store chain Blockbuster dominated the movie rental market. Little towns, suburbs, big cities all had Blockbusters. The company grew and expanded, and it gave its customers what they wanted: a wide selection of movies right in their backyard. In 2010, Blockbuster filed for bankruptcy. Why? Because the Netflix business model of mailing DVDs to viewers and streaming movies over the internet had eroded so much of Blockbuster's business that it could no longer sustain itself. In the year 2000, a company like Netflix would have been unthinkable. Mailing DVDs would have sounded silly and the infrastructure required to stream video was out of reach. And what about the human touch? Did we want to have a person on hand to help us? If you asked Blockbuster customers, they probably would have told you that browsing in the local store was an important experience. They definitely would not have asked for streaming video, and why would they want to wait three or four days to get a DVD in the mail when they could just walk down the street and pick one up off the shelf? Blockbuster died not because it didn't do its job well, but because it didn't recognize that the world was changing around it. Netflix was not better at being Blockbuster. Netflix was a whole new thing (Surowicki, 2010).

That said, I do not think that libraries are the next Blockbuster. Librarians do recognize that the world is changing around them, which is why they have jumped into social media with both feet. The reality is that social media are no longer new. "Blog" was the word of the year in 2004 (BBC News, 2004), so it's not like we haven't had enough time to evaluate the technology. Not only have many libraries evaluated social media, but many have escalated its use to all parts of their existence. At the same time, there are still significant numbers of libraries that barely have a basic website up and running.

This book is an argument for making social media fit your library. Although I may dabble in some of the hype around social media, I do not believe social media to be the answer to all of the challenges facing libraries. Some aspects of our work have not changed over the past decade, and some aspects will not change over the next decade. Our users will always have a need for information, a need for community space, a need for open and affordable learning, and, ultimately, a need for us to engage our community for the betterment of all. The model for how we fill these needs may shift, but the needs will remain.

The argument here is that social media in your library must make sense for your library. For some of us, that may mean pulling back. For others, it may mean scaling up. For all of us it is about weighing needs and resources and considering how our staff members work as an organization, because this book is not really about technology at all. It is about people, interaction and engagement.

A note about terminology

I generally use the phrase *social media* to refer to a broad range of specific technologies including blogs, microblogs, social networking sites, social bookmarking sites, video sharing and location-based sites. In some places, I may discuss a specific type of technology (e.g. microblogging) and where appropriate I discuss specific tools (e.g. Twitter). Experts debate whether or not these tools are really related technologies deserving to be classified together. I acknowledge this, although the debate is not carried forward in this text. Many of these technologies are banded together because they are part of a wave of innovation that is different from preceding tools. Only time will tell whether the concept of social media carries meaning into the future. As the concepts in this text can be applied across a range of social tools, the practical implications for the technology do not hinge on whether these tools are classified together.

In the text, I refer to the people who work in libraries. For the sake of practicality, I often refer to these people in general terms. Our profession is quite diverse in how we employ people to accomplish work. Depending on country, type of library, size of community, size of budgets, contractual obligations and goals, we ask people with different levels of training to perform many different (and similar) tasks. I generally use the term *librarian* to refer to individuals with a master's degree in library and information science who perform the central functions of the library profession. I use the phrases *library staff* or *organizational members* to refer to any employee, including librarians, who work in a library. I leave it to the reader to translate the ideas of this text into their specific library environment.

About the author

Troy A. Swanson is Teaching & Learning Librarian and Library Department Chair at Moraine Valley Community College in the USA. Troy earned his PhD from Old Dominion University in Norfolk, Virginia and his master's degree in library and information science from Dominican University in River Forest, Illinois. His BA is from Augustana College in Rock Island, Illinois.

Troy interviewed at Moraine Valley in the year 2000 as a practice interview in preparation for opportunities at larger universities. He fell in love with the open-access mission of American community colleges and is committed to the ideal that higher education should be accessible and affordable to all. Troy has managed the Moraine Valley Library's web presence since 2000. He implemented his library's blogs in 2004 using a content management approach and the library's first podcasts for cultural events in 2006. His work on library website design and usability has been published in the *Journal of Academic Librarianship* and *Internet Reference Services Quarterly*. Troy also writes as a guest contributor on the *Tame the Web* blog. His PhD dissertation focused on the management of Web 2.0 in higher education. He has also written on information literacy instruction for college students.

Troy and his wife Kim live outside of Chicago with their three children Skylar, Parker and Lainey. They love their local public library and spend a great deal of time riding their bikes to utilize its resources. Recently, Troy and Kim surrendered the last vestiges of their former urban existence and embraced suburban life by purchasing a minivan.

The author may be contacted at:

Troy A. Swanson
Moraine Valley Community College Library
9000 W. College Pkwy
Palos Hills
IL 60465
USA

Tel: +1 708 974 5439
Email: *swanson@morainevalley.edu*
Twitter: *https://twitter.com/#!/T_Swanson*

Where have we been with social media?

Abstract: Social media simplify the technological side of the web but complicate the people side because now any library staff member can publish information. Librarians have experience with a range of social media tools, but the challenge lies in aligning organizational needs with those tools. As the web has gained prominence, people are increasingly overloaded with information. Filtering and searching are two options for managing this overload. Searching has dominated, but filtering via social media is set to become the next phase in the development of the web. Now that librarians have had experience with many social media tools, they can step back and refocus their use of social media.

Key words: social media, libraries, user attention, filtering, searching, information overload, organizational focus

Introduction

Most libraries are beyond the coming-to-grips stage with social media. We have implemented blogs, dived into MySpace, tagged sites in Delicious, jumped over to Facebook, let our MySpace pages die, uploaded video to YouTube, tagged photos in Flickr, started tweeting, messed with Tumblr, and started pages on Google+. Whether we liked it or not, we have managed social media, or, at least, people in our organizations have experimented with social media. We have bravely met the technological challenge of engaging and initiating social media. *We get social media.* We have solved the technology.

Believe it or not, technology problems tend to be solved with money and time. (Clearly, money and time are not always in surplus.) Unfortunately, most problems are not purely technical. Libraries are human enterprises, and technology problems pale in comparison to human problems as they tend to constantly shift and grow. Technology tends to have a few, defined purposes and functions, but we call on people to work in many areas and deal with a range of functions. Maybe it is more accurate to say that technology problems are solvable, while we hope to make human problems manageable.

It follows then that managing social media is not really about the social media. These tools are not complicated in the same way that learning DOS was in the 1980s. DOS was a whole new world that had its own logic and language. Most of us went from not having a computer at all to having to navigate DOS. But, this is not what we are facing with social media. The world wide web really gained mass prominence in the late 1990s, so we have lived with the web for many years. Social media represent an extension of something familiar. Social media have become a feature that we never knew we wanted, but now that we have it, we can't live without it. Social media represent the microwave oven of the web. We never asked for it, but now that we have it, we will never heat up leftovers on the stove-top again. We get it, and we can't possibly go back.

Managing social media in libraries is absolutely a people problem and absolutely not a technology problem. Managing social media for people is not really different from managing social media for a person. Whether we are talking about one person or 20 people, we must keep track of sites, user names and passwords. Most importantly, they need an awareness of who is using the site and how they are connecting with them. We need to understand how various sites connect users and how information is shared between users. When I post information to a site, who sees it? Does everybody or does one person? Are my posts available to people who are not members of the network? Could someone find it through a Google search?

When I go to Google+, I know that the members of the moms' group to which my wife belongs tend to dominate my feed. They all have migrated away from Facebook and onto Google+. When I post on Google+, I have to be careful not to say things that will get me in trouble with my wife and her friends (although I do sometimes post things just to get them up in arms). On the other hand, my primary concern on Facebook is that my own, real-life mom does not find embarrassing college photos of me posted by my old college roommates. At the same time, I use Twitter, Ning and Delicious for professional activities. In all cases, I try to make myself aware of available privacy settings and who is using the sites in order to connect personally and professionally. Of course, there are many tools that I choose not use at all.

Two questions must be addressed in using social media: *how will a particular tool be useful for me* and *what information will I choose to share?* Whether you are an individual signing up for Facebook for the first time or an organization of 100 people using Delicious to curate links, the questions are essentially the same. How is this useful? What will we share? Of course, answering these two questions in an organizational context is a bit more complicated than answering for an individual.

What happens when two staff members see issues differently? How do we address different needs through the same tools? Many social media platforms are based on individual users. They are very public, and they easily co-mingle personal usage and professional usage. When a library user interacts with our library on a social media site, we do not want to appear to be erratic with many librarians posting on every topic under the sun. However, we also want users to experience the richness hidden within the many personalities who work in our libraries. We do not want to appear erratic, but we also do not want to have a bland, corporate voice.

This means that our organizational members need direction when using social media. Conversations need to occur around why we are using these tools and how we are using these tools. We must examine how we are connected to each other, which means that social media do not just help libraries connect with the external world. Social media also help our staff members connect with each other. When managing social media, we must understand how tools can be useful and what we want to share, but we also must recognize that there are internal uses for social media tools and external uses for these tools. A big part of managing social media in an organizational context is recognizing and taking advantage of the internal/external divide.

Filtering vs searching

We link, post, share, like, feed and send. We have feeds, aggregators, email alerts, personalized news sites, text alerts, wall posts and timeline posts. It has become clichéd to say that information overload is all around us. We like to show off that over 80 percent of the population in Western Europe and the USA have internet access (World Bank, 2010), that our species has the capacity to store over 295 exabytes of information (Hilbert and López, 2011), or that there are over a billion chat sessions per day on Facebook (Parr, 2009). We are immersed in a flow of information that has escaped from the desktop and now follows us on mobile devices. But this flow has not just taken over our hardware—it has taken over our minds. The constant conversation and connections have implanted themselves in our brains. It's not about numbers of sites or access rates. The information overload manifests as a constant need to keep up.

I am surely an information addict. I can't resist. On my drive to work, there is one long stoplight where I inevitably sit and wait. No matter what time I leave home, I end up waiting through several cycles of the light as traffic moves forward. Sometimes it feels like it takes forever, and while I wait, I just can't resist glancing at my phone to see if any new email messages have arrived since I pulled out of my garage. I know it is dangerous, but how can I not look? My phone calls to me. Try as I may, I can't help but just glancing at my inbox or my Twitter feed. "OK, I won't actually read anything," I tell myself, "but if I can just take a peak to see what new things have popped up ... Just to give me a head start when I get to the parking lot." I feel the constant pressure to keep the information tidal wave at bay, the need to read one message and delete it before the next message arrives.

Clearly, my strategy may not be the best to follow, but it does show some of the dangers of the information onslaught. All of us work to find ways to keep up. In *The Information*, James Gleick (2011) tells us that people use two primary strategies people for handling the information glut: filtering and searching.

Searching identifies specific content based on a specific need. Search has dominated the web from its earliest days. The problem of seeking information in an effective way was certainly the central problem of the web in the 1990s. Of course, Google showed us how to do it, and now search is almost second nature. What would the web be without search, or, more specifically, without Google?

Search has become the language of the web, but with social media, filtering is quickly catching up. Social media include some of our most effective filtering tools. With social media, we filter information for each other. Twitter is my favorite filtering tool. I follow people who post links to sites, articles and videos that match my interests. I review the tweets in my feed and save the links that catch my eye. This type of filtering is happening in Facebook, Google+, and many other sites. Content creators add buttons on sites to make it easier for readers to push pages out into the social media stream. The social media site Digg has built its business model around filtering.

But social media have not just allowed us to socialize articles and web pages but also to connect the virtual world with our physical world. We are filtering restaurants, parks, homes and schools. There is an entire cadre of social media tools such as Foursquare, Facebook Places and many others that use the GPS capabilities in mobile devices to allow users to recommend services, identify special events, or play location-based games.

Search may have dominated the web in the first years of the twenty-first century, but filtering is transforming how the web works and how we interact with our world. In 2011, Google, the dominant force in searching, launched its social media site, Google+; now it is working to socialize search so that filtering and search cross. Of course, significant numbers of people must participate in order for social media to have impact. Search can exist in a single-to-many relationship, which is typically a Google-to-everyone relationship. Social media, on the other hand, require a many-to-many relationship. Twitter would be nowhere near as useful were there only two users. Part of the thrill and bane of Facebook is that all of your old school classmates are on it. In order for it to work, we all have to participate.

In some ways, social media are fulfilling the promise of the web. In the mid-1990s, the web promised to democratize information and publishing. Everyone could "publish" information. We could bypass the gatekeepers. It didn't take us very long to figure out that big companies had cool sites, and most individuals had clunky, unattractive sites (Blood, 2002). Sure, we could make a page on Geocities, and we had email, but we couldn't put out information with polish. That is, until the turn of the century when the first wave of blogging sites hit the web. Blogs were the first social media tool that broke into the popular consciousness, and they were the first significant tool that allowed the average person to publish information with ease. They required no knowledge of HTML, no page management, and no hosting fees. If one wanted to get fancy, one could purchase a domain name, but that wasn't a requirement. Even today, blogs still make up the backbone of much social media use. They were, and are, one of the original filtering tools.

Librarians should not be strangers to searching or filtering. We have been doing both for centuries. Obviously, the card catalog is all about searching. We spent the better part of the twentieth century developing subject headings and debating "aboutness." MARC allowed us to scale our work as never before. Up to around 1998, we were arguably the masters of search. Creating searching tools and instructing users on using those tools was our primary business.

Of course, we do spend some time filtering. Collection development, when done correctly, is essentially a large filtering effort to meet the needs of the local community.

Collection development is a matter of economics and user need. Librarians select specific information sources out of the universe of all sources. After an item is selected, it is processed and made searchable—and a great deal of library resources are devoted to preparing items for search. With collection development as our primary filtering service, reference services are focused less on filtering than on searching. Perhaps we perform some filtering by creating some finding aides, making some book displays, and organizing clipping services. But we really spend most of our time thinking about searching.

The web and social media have changed all of this. Now, everyone filters, and every library *should* filter. Yet it's not enough just to collect and organize—we are also growing increasingly social. Libraries have a role to play as participants in socializing information. We can highlight information sources that are part of our own collections or sources that are on the web. We can bring users together—virtually or in person—to add comments or reviews. We can make cultural events in the library extend beyond our walls and live on after the event has ended. We can find ways to reach out into our communities and participate.

Attention is expensive, while storage is cheap

When I was working on my master's degree, I worked for a short time at one of Northwestern University's small branch libraries in downtown Chicago. As I was a graduate student, I tended to get stuck with the Saturday morning shift, which was slow and allowed me to catch up on classwork. Each Saturday, a small, frail-looking older gentleman would creep into the library. He'd remove his battered fedora and pick up the morning's *New York Times*. Then, carefully, he would examine each page of the newspaper. Looking them up and down, he would carefully turn each page, licking his thumb once in a while to ensure that pages didn't stick together.

At that time, I had more readings than I could manage. I would pile books and copies of articles into my backpack so that I could read during slow times at the reference desk. Many times, I would be pulling up articles online and bookmarking websites to visit later. When I watched the older man come in and read the *New York Times*, I felt that I was sneaking a glimpse of bygone days. He had *one* source before him. He read methodically. When he was done, he neatly folded up the paper in a very respectful, but also physical way. He returned it to its proper place and then strolled out of the library. I knew that I did not read like this. Not only did I not have the time to read like this, but I also didn't have the attention span. I just couldn't sit and look at every section of a newspaper. It was so linear. My mind couldn't operate like this.

There was a time when people had time to read. Late eighteenth and nineteenth-century novels were long and flowing. Letters were formal and wordy. The creation and distribution of information were slow and expensive so information sources arrived sporadically, one at a time. Getting information was a geographic exercise. Times have changed. Now, the moment of birth initiates a digital information flow that never stops. Content flows easily and relatively cheaply. Thomas Jefferson was well known as a major book purchaser. It was not an exaggeration to say that he physically owned a significant portion of the information of his day (Jefferson, Gilreath and Wilson, 1989). Today, no one can come anywhere near this claim. We are bombarded with information with ever-shifting attention.

In the late sixteenth and through the seventeenth century, England felt the shocks of an information revolution brought on by the availability of print. During the reign of Henry VIII, around 80 publications a year were printed and distributed. By the start of the English Civil War a century later, the publication mark hit 2000 a year. This annual figure would double during the war. Leading up to the war, print allowed British readers to be connected to the rest of Europe as never before. They followed the conflicts between and within France and Spain over Protestantism, a topic that directly impacted local English politics. During the war, print reflected and exacerbated political division. This was one of those times in history where we could see communities form because of an information technology. Individuals did not need to be geographically together, but created movements from a distance through sharing ideas. Pseudo-newspapers had been in existence prior to the war, but it was the use of print through the war that established printed news as a key mechanism in society.

Before the Civil War, the government of Charles I did not have an official newspaper but was instead represented by advocates in print. This meant that their voices were mixed up in the tumult. After the Restoration, however, the government of Charles II could not ignore print in this way and had an official newspaper that spoke loudly above any debate. From this point forward, newspapers became a primary means of discourse. Their use spread quickly as they were carried around the world.

Print, as a new information technology, wedged its way into the existing information ecosystem. When print first arrived, people read out loud and in groups because only a fraction of the population could read. An oral news network already existed and print injected itself into it. Although it initially enhanced oral culture, print eventually stopped being a tool to help one person share news with another; instead, it became a tool for people to receive their own news. Print shifted culture as it extended knowledge to the masses as never before. By today's standards, literacy rates remained low for centuries to come, but the impact of print was widespread and truly revolutionary. It grew during a time of political controversy and allowed for the articulation of new ideas by new voices (Hughes, 1998; Sharpe, 2000).

If we really want to stretch back to before the printing press, it is arguable that the oldest social networking tool was the letter. As literacy and writing spread, the use and impact of letters to connect social hubs across time and space grew. From St. Paul to Mary Shelley, epistolary writing was a standard literary form. Scholars from Stanford's "Mapping the Republic of Letters" project (*https://republicofletters. stanford.edu/*) are exploring the social networks between leading thinkers across Europe and mapping the hubs of knowledge that connected England to the continent. Every century has its own information revolution and all of them can be measured in terms of the information volume, speed of delivery, and social connections they fostered.

The ease and immediacy of information sharing in the early twenty-first century highlight the impact of our own information technology revolutions. Examples include the post-election protests in Iran in 2009, dubbed the "Twitter Revolution," and the "Arab Spring" of 2011, the organization of which relied heavily on Facebook and YouTube. Information has been removed from physical boundaries and sent around the world digitally.

In the past, when information had to be embodied in a physical format, we could stumble upon information sources. The day's newspaper was delivered to the door. The weekly magazine lay on the coffee table. The new novel waited patiently on the nightstand next to the bed. Although these formats have not vanished, they are now interrupted by the buzzes and beeps of new messages and new comments. The link found in a tweet leads to a blog post which leads to a

Wikipedia entry. Sources are skimmed and left behind for the next discovery. No longer do we read them in their entirety and allow time for contemplation.

Over the centuries we have gone from information scarcity to an information surplus beyond our wildest dreams. Everyone has become a writer, a publisher, a photographer, videographer, and, of course, a critic. Attention is today's currency. It is a commodity in limited supply, expended nugget by nugget. We are a society that has engaged in a battle for eyeballs. Business models revolve around attracting those eyeballs. Whether selling information to users or giving away information while selling advertising, the bottom line is engaging users in content.

The driving force behind much of this is cheap information storage. Users can easily access sites via the web, and sites can store and organize data at relatively little cost. Sites run different software and offer different services but their central point is the same, which is to allow users to create and deposit data at no cost to the user. *Wired* magazine's Chris Anderson (2009) tells us that "free" is the new norm. Sites give away their services knowing that a vast majority of their visitors will give them nothing but may visit a few ads on their site. These sites also hope that a minority of visitors will be willing to pay for expanded services, and those payments will be enough to support the entire site. The model is to give away 90 percent—or more—of the service with the hope that 10 percent will be enough to make a profit. In order to seek out that 10 percent, the battle for attention is being waged.

The media and faculty at business schools are making a big deal about the willingness of sites to give away information and services for free as if this is a new invention. They fail to mention that libraries have been doing this for centuries. We have been making information and a range of services available to our communities. Most libraries have done this as publicly-supported entities. We have had educational missions seeking to be community learning centers. This is our advantage. The web in general, but social media in particular, offers an opportunity to extend our services. We must remain true to our missions and strive to be efficient with public resources as we serve our communities. We also must recognize that serving the public good is our competitive advantage. There are many information services the market will not make freely available, and we must be prepared to fill in the gaps.

Naturally, as we join the battle for attention, we must also remember that attention is expensive for our libraries too. Even during the best of times, budgets are limited. It is not possible to meet all user demand, and it is impossible for libraries to participate in every social media site. Our organizations have limited attention. Managers and organizational leaders must help to direct this attention.

Time to step back and refocus

Our staff time is our most valuable resource. Needs grow, but staffing does not keep pace. Each day, new social networking tools hit the scene. Either we decide not to try them out because we simply cannot handle another username and password, or we jump in and add the new site to our list of 30 other sites that we must update each day. A blog post, Facebook update, Google+ update and tweet follow any change of services by our libraries. This may also mean that following any committee meeting, three or four staff members may choose to share information on behalf of your library. On top of this, when staff members go home, they may be posting work-related information to their personal social media networks. We are not so much connected via a gossamer web of finely tuned communication channels as by a knotted ball of yarn.

We have now hit a point in the history of social networking where we can step back and refocus. Social networking is no longer brand new. Our staff members have had experience using these tools. Some new tools come and go, but many tools, such as Blogger, Wordpress, YouTube, Delicious and others, have been around for years. Managers can direct the attention of organizational members and clearly connect social media tools to organizational goals. They may not recognize exactly how this connection is to be made, but they can initiate a process where staff members can work together to discover how these connections should work.

Our organization members have some big picture needs that must be addressed. First, there is a need for clear messages communicated via social media. This may not mean a single voice or a "corporate" voice. However, messages should support brand identity and the organization's marketing push. Second, participants can benefit from clear workflows where everyone involved understands their role and how they can participate. Third, defined workflows should push for a degree of efficiency in how and what tools are used. Fourth, the organization as a whole needs protection from the potential mistakes of members, and members need protection in their own use of social media tools.

Finally, Web 2.0 also presents an opportunity for us to capture and share the knowledge that members of our organization create as they do their jobs. It's not just an opportunity to do new things, but also an opportunity to become better at the things that we have always done. It could be as simple as a blog post following a complicated reference interview, or a series of tweets to build awareness as cultural events are organized. In the end, we can become better at connecting patrons to information and to our services.

2

Library organizations as loosely-coupled systems

Abstract: Libraries are made of up people who must coordinate their work in order to use resources and manage tasks efficiently. Like all organizations, libraries use coordination tools to get this done. Coordination tools include policies, budgets, organizational culture and participation rules. As a library's outcomes are not directly connected to resources, processes are not directly related, and user interactions vary greatly, libraries operate as loosely-coupled systems. As loosely-coupled systems, libraries enjoy a flexibility and an ability to innovate, but also must account for weaknesses such as inefficiencies and a difficulty in instituting change.

Key words: social media, libraries, loosely-coupled systems, policies, budgets, participation rules, organizational culture, coordination tools

Introduction

It is easy for us to talk about our "library" as if it is alive. I catch myself doing this all the time in meetings: "the library will take responsibility for planning the speakers series" or "the library made 10 000 periodicals available through a new database." Perhaps it is healthy to think of our libraries as living, breathing entities that take action and assert themselves into the lives of our community. If we don't believe that libraries are alive, then who will?

Yet, as managers and leaders, we must recognize that our libraries do not really exist. Sure, we have buildings, we have information sources, we have technology infrastructures, and we have people. But, our library really never does anything. When action is taken, it is taken by a person. When a patron calls a reference desk, the library does not answer the phone—a librarian does. When the library purchases a book or subscribes to a new database, a person (or people) makes the selection, other people sign the checks, and others process the new resource. In our minds, we envision a single entity that must evolve and grow to remain relevant to those whom we serve. But, in reality, we should picture a group of people who sometimes step forward together and sometimes step sideways right into each other. In fact, many times we are bumbling and bumping our way forward. And, yes, sometimes we are bumbling and bumping our way backward.

Coordination tools

This begs the question, how does this group of individuals work together to reduce the bumbling and bumping? The difference between a group of people just milling about looking up information and a group of people who are actually organized is the ability to coordinate their actions. The reason we coordinate is to divide up tasks effectively and allow individuals to accomplish pieces of the task. In a practical sense, coordination revolves around the use of coordination tools. There are four basic types of coordination tool that should be familiar to all of us in modern organizations: policies, participation rules, budgets and culture. Coordination tools allow people to work toward goals. Ideally, they allow us to work efficiently.

All of us are regularly affected by these tools, but we rarely think about what they do for us. Without coordination tools, each morning we would have to sit down with our staff members and decide not only who would do each job, but also what jobs needed to be done, the rules around accomplishing all of our work, and methods for reporting on our work. We would be starting at step one every day. It would be inefficient, and most likely nothing would be accomplished.

In the late 1990s, I was lucky enough to start a brand new library for the Presidio Trust in San Francisco, California (Figure 2.1). There were two of us working for a new government entity that managed the buildings of the former army base right on the Golden Gate. It was one of the world's most scenic spots, with the Pacific on one side, the San Francisco Bay on the other, and the city of San Francisco right out the door. Of course, we spent most of our time inside with boxes of books, land use assessments and environmental impact studies. We started at ground zero,

Figure 2.1   Presidio of San Francisco Coast Guard Station

writing policy, ordering software, putting items on shelves, organizing furniture, and generally figuring out what it actually meant to coordinate our actions with the goals of the larger organization. Most days literally started with trying to figure out what needed to be done next. In the early days, we accomplished very few substantive tasks because we had to spend so much time figuring out what the substantive tasks were. This was a necessarily slow and difficult process, but we had little choice. In most libraries, the person who opens in the morning has a well-defined opening procedure. When additional employees show up for work, they step right in and start their daily tasks. It is rare that much conversation needs to happen in order to figure out what should happen next. We have schedules, job assignments and rules that allow us to get work done. We have coordination tools to allow us to understand our work and know how to do it.

In fact, one absolutely vital part of coordination tools is to make work predictable in two ways. First, employees need predictability in their work so that they can plan their work in both the short and long term, understand how their role relates to others, recognize how they will be evaluated so that they can improve, and retain a degree of sanity in their lives. Different jobs include different degrees of certainty and uncertainty. We rarely want jobs to be too predictable because we grow bored with them. However, we also do not necessarily want an erratic work life where the possibilities of success are constantly shifting beneath us.

The second reason that we need coordination tools to make work predictable is because we are offering a service that we hope has some degree of quality. Managers and leaders have a general goal that when presented with similar situations, different employees will take similar actions. We want our employees to understand the goals of the organization and how to act toward those goals. Our libraries are open days, nights and weekends. Our goal should be that our users will be treated and given access to our services in a similar way no matter the time of day or the person sitting behind the service desk. While we recognize that our librarians are not robots programmed to take exact action in specific situations, we also have expectations for quality of service. Coordination tools act as the mechanism within in the organization to maintain service levels and organize work.

What are coordination tools?

The coordination tools that we think of most often probably come in the form of policies. Policies come in all sizes and flavors, but they are generally written. They also tend to be more formal. Policies attempt to codify action, values and approach. They are the most clear attempt to make the implicit something more explicit. Policies include strategic plans, missions, core values, operational policies and written procedures. Ideally, they offer staff members guidance when faced with particular problems. What is your library's policy on food and drink? What is your library's policy on children using computers in the adult services area? What is your policy on materials selection? They might not admit it, but most staff members actually like policies. Policies offer clarity. If there is a problem, let's just write a new policy and fix it. Of course, most of us would rather have a hot poker stabbed into our eye socket than read a policy handbook. Most managers and leaders know that policies are rarely read and that policies alone solve few problems. Nonetheless, they are often necessary, and when implemented in the right ways, can have impact.

Budgets, on the other hand, almost always have impact. Budgets are the essential allocation of resources across the organization. We generally think about money when we think about budgets, but budgets are really about numbers of people, furniture and physical space. If you want to understand the priorities of organizational leaders, take a look at the budget. Money doesn't solve all problems, but it sure doesn't hurt. Budgets are an essential coordination tool because they formalize resources distribution between areas and try to balance needs. Often, they are a big part of deciding what gets done.

Perhaps the most overarching coordination tool is culture. It is so big that we may debate whether or not it actually counts as a "tool." Culture includes the informal rules and human interactions that fill in the gaps between the formal tools. As soon as the first human joins the organization, culture takes shape. The organizational culture defines how people interact with each other. It includes values, purpose and informal rules of interaction. New employees begin being indoctrinated into the culture on day one. Policies may outline formal rewards and reprimands, but culture defines the informal rewards and reprimands, which often turn out to be more motivating. Library managers may not have written a formal policy about parking in the very first parking spot right next to the staff entrance, but everyone knows that this spot belongs to library director and those who dare to park in it will suffer. Culture revolves around symbols, influence and inter-personal connections. I believe that culture counts as a coordination "tool" because it can be used for change. Culture can be difficult and unwieldy, but it can be molded over time. Culture makes many things possible that could never be written out as policy.

Participation rules are the last coordination tool. This is another one that some may question as a "tool," because participation rules are actually a combination of the other tools. In terms of managing social media, participation rules warrant their own consideration. Participation rules define who gets to do what. They are not just about division of labor, but about the degree of autonomy each individual has within the larger group. Participation rules are defined by formal policies, but they go beyond policies. They also are guided by culture at a day-to-day level. However, we cannot just say that they are the same thing as organizational culture because they are bit more formal. Budgets play a part in this by setting up what managers "own" what resources and how they can dictate action. Participation rules combine formal and informal to form a decision-making structure. Individuals who really understand their organization recognize how to work within this structure to get things done.

On my campus, computer lab space is at a premium. Our library has two computer labs intended for information literacy instruction. If a faculty member wants to work with a librarian, any librarian can schedule these labs for any time of the semester. The labs are set aside for instruction, and the librarians are empowered to utilize these rooms for this service. If a faculty member wants to use one of our labs as an open lab without a librarian, he or she can reserve the room within 24 hours notice just by calling the librarian at our information desk. If an instructor wants to reserve the lab 25 hours from now, it can't happen. However, savvy departmental secretaries and faculty members know that, as library department chair, I have the authority to bypass this rule. Individuals who understand the participation rules know that they can work around the formal structure by calling me. Of course, most of the time I tell them to get lost, but they still try. My librarians recognize that this is not their decision, and they know that they know that it will be a breach in policy to do this.

Thus, the most essential decision for any employee in any organization is to decide whether or not a choice is their choice to make. When faced with a situation, each staff member must decide whether they need to consult with a supervisor or whether the action is their own. This can include a complex calculus accounting for positive and negative repercussions. Sometimes this may take the form of a library user asking us to bend a rule, and sometimes this may take the form of an employee subtly (or not so subtly) pushing us to do something. We consider the consequences of our actions. Sometimes we take action, and sometimes we go to our boss for guidance or permission. Most of the time, we may not consider this, because most of the decisions we make are very clear. But gray areas do arise. Then we have to figure out how to make decisions. During leadership changes, reorganizations, times of great growth, times of cutbacks, or implementation of new technologies participation rules may change and decision-making might become tricky business for employees. A key part of being in any organization is understanding when a decision belongs to you and when it does not.

The library as loosely-coupled system

A challenge that our organizations face is that we offer services that produce a variety of results. A reference interaction can be highly personalized, and the decisions made by our staff members require significant judgment. There is often a disconnection between types of results and the actions required to reach those results. For this reason, it is useful to think of our libraries as "loosely-coupled systems." Loose systems in organizational terms were defined by organizational psychologist Karl Weick (1976). Weick argues that we should move away from rational models of organizations that emphasize inputs and outputs towards organizations that are people based. His model considers how individuals make sense of their jobs using coordination tools. He states:

> If one looks for an organization, one will not find it. What will be found is that there are events, linked together, that transpire with concrete walls and these sequences, their pathways, their timing, are the forms we erroneously make into substances when we talk about an organization. (Weick, 1974: 358)

Perhaps, loosely-coupled systems can be best understood by contrasting them with tightly-coupled systems. The classic example of a tight system is an assembly line where the finished product is directly tied to exact steps in the process. Weick (1982) outlines four traits of tightly-coupled systems. First, they have rules. Second, people agree on the rules. Third, there is a system of inspection to judge the fulfillment of these rules. Finally, there is feedback to improve the process. If the car frame is not properly constructed early in the assembly line, then there will be problems attaching the doors later on in the process.

In loosely-coupled systems, at least one of the four traits described above is missing. It can be very difficult to see a process and identify how specific inputs affect outcomes. What percentage of student learning is impacted by my library on my college campus? I am sure it varies widely by student. I know that some students are greatly impacted by our library, that other students do not use our resources at all, and a large number of students fall somewhere in between.

For most libraries, "looseness" occurs in three ways. First, there is a looseness around connecting outcomes to resources. When we increase something like our materials budget or add staff members, we struggle to measure the direct increase in service to our community. What is the exact improvement for each hour of staff time that is added? I have no idea. We try to measure value by showing usage of facilities and getting feedback from users, but connecting inputs and outputs is tough. Increasing inputs by a specific amount does not result in a specific percentage of increased output.

Second, there is a looseness in defining the interactions with users. Some users enter our libraries with very specific and well-defined needs. Others come to see us with a vague idea of their goals and desires. We must adapt our services to meet the needs of the people standing before us. We might use coordination tools to define services and ensure equity of access to services, but most of our services require staff members to adapt resources to the unique needs that arise each day. This means that we cannot standardize what we do. It also means that our services must remain flexible, or we risk underserving users.

Finally, there is a range of looseness and tightness within our own processes. Some processes are tight. Others are loose. The process behind materials acquisition is more than likely much tighter than the process behind reference. Ordering a database requires a tightness in decision making, creating requisition orders, transferring funds and implementing on a website. Subscribing to one database may mean that other resources must be given up, and it may mean that processing of other resources must wait. In contrast, answering a reference question involves a high degree of variability. There may be a system behind reference that involves preparation, scheduling and capturing knowledge, but this is a very loose process. The outcome of one reference question will more than likely have little impact on other reference questions even though the knowledge gained from one question may help with future questions.

Strengths and weaknesses of loosely-coupled systems

As with most things, loosely-coupled systems have strengths and weaknesses. The weaknesses of loose systems are that they are inefficient by nature and difficult to manage. They are by nature inefficient because, as mentioned above, it is difficult to connect inputs and outputs. When we add more resources or expand services, it is difficult to know which ones will be the most successful in helping users. A resource may be underutilized for many months, and then, for no clear reason, usage numbers may skyrocket. Matching a community with resources, programming and learning opportunities cannot be accomplished via formula.

The result of this looseness is that managers and leaders are presented with challenges. First, defining how a process or service actually works can be difficult. Our services are tied together. When usage numbers for a particular resource skyrocket, it may be due to a local community group using a meeting room, so the right people were in the library at the right time. Recognizing this is often impossible. Another challenge for managers is recognizing what counts as waste and what degree of inefficiency is just part of the service. The most significant challenge with loose systems is creating feedback loops that channel data and information back into the system for improvement.

Change can be difficult and slow in loose systems. As mentioned above, staff members rely on some degree of predictability in order to split up their work. When staff members do not get clear feedback from the system, they often default to predictability and do not recognize opportunities for change. Managers can be positioned to recognize the big picture and push for change, but they too find it difficult to get useful data and information to really know where to make changes. When connections between outcomes and inputs are fuzzy, then change becomes difficult on all levels.

Of course, the strength of loose systems is that they are very flexible. Libraries demonstrate a high degree of flexibility. We may have trouble measuring outcomes, but we also have a freedom to experiment. As one area of the library is only loosely connected to another, this experimentation can occur in pockets without harming the entire organization. We can explore a range of possibilities and adaptations without requiring the entire system to be reorganized. When loosely-coupled systems are at their best, subunits identify innovation and communicate innovations back across the organization for adoption.

For example, if your library does not use the photo-sharing site Flickr, the staff who organize public events might try it as a way to share and show off events. After they have used it a few times, they start to become the local Flickr experts. When the library director wants to use it to promote the visit by a prominent elected official, then they can ask for support from the local experts. In this way, loosely-coupled systems have a high capacity for storing a variety of innovations for ever-shifting needs in the environment. Of course, the difficulty is knowing how to locate these pockets of expertise, which is why sharing and transparency become important.

This view of our libraries as organizations is valuable when we consider social media tools. Libraries do not operate as monolithic hierarchies where top-down orders produce standardized actions. Our libraries employ a diversity of people working in largely decentralized ways to serve our patrons. Our libraries are centers of rich creativity that offer flexible and adaptive services. As we consider social media tools, we must consider how the tools emphasize our strengths and how they address our weaknesses.

3

Social media in loosely-coupled systems

Abstract: As loosely-coupled systems, libraries can use social media tools to strengthen their advantages. Librarians can use social media tools to capture knowledge, collaborate, extend their marketing, give staff and users a voice, and connect the virtual world to the physical world. Librarians must be aware of the disintermediation of traditional media caused by disruptive technologies. Library leaders must allow their libraries to remain flexible enough to adapt while tightening their loose system to share information and collaborate.

Key words: social media, libraries, loosely-coupled systems, collaboration, capturing knowledge, empowering staff, empowering users, marketing, disintermediation

Introduction

Recently, our early-morning librarian told me that she has never met two of our evening librarians. One of our weekend librarians has worked for us for over two decades, and I am sure that many of our weekday librarians have never met her. We are an organization of people who are never all together. We do not work next to each other. We do not get face-to-face opportunities to solve problems together. If every librarian worked side-by-side, then librarians would observe each other and create shared experiences around services. Over time, this would create informal standards and approaches. Were change needed, managers could more easily take action. Alas, this is not how we operate. Instead, we rely on communication channels such as emails, policies and meeting notes to share information. Managers conduct evaluations and professional development for staff that (we hope) create a shared vision and approach to our work. We establish processes that allow us to share knowledge and review our work. When procedures change, managers must work to ensure that staff are aware and following the change. A great degree of coordination between staff members falls on the shoulders of managers. Obviously, this is the role of management, but lack of direct contact between organizational members exacerbates this challenge.

Over the years, I have worked with my library staff to implement a number of social media tools. In so doing, I have considered how tools complement our organization as a loosely-coupled system. Of course, what makes social media "social" is their ability to connect people. Their connections can take on many forms, but their essence is tying together people in online communication. This means connecting individuals inside and beyond library walls, connecting people to events and happenings, and connecting people to the organization. A useful internal/external divide exists in connecting organizational members to each other and to people outside of the organization. Internal needs are largely about communicating and capturing knowledge while external needs are largely about extending services.

Internal: capturing knowledge

Every day, librarians and staff members make discoveries. They find ways to be more efficient. They solve difficult issues for patrons. They fix, they find and they invent. Our staff members are truly interdisciplinary, naturally curious and amazingly creative. As much of the work we do is loosely coupled to the work of others, curiosity is often our true business. When we explore that unique reference question, we are required to be thoughtful and imaginative. Anyone who has worked at a reference desk is well aware that reference is not really about searching. It is often about defining the problem with users and considering the degree of credibility required to answer the question.

Social media have the potential to capture knowledge that does not get captured via formal means. This is the knowledge that we stumble upon when working side-by-side with someone. This is the knowledge that no one could possibly recognize as valuable. Staff members can post this information as a means of sharing. The key is not for staff members to guess what other people need. They should just share things that they think are worthy of note and let others utilize this knowledge.

The reference transaction is an obvious source of knowledge creation, but there are other service needs that result in discoveries. This could be the newly developed workaround for the "upgrade" to the library system, the use of a new process for withdrawing items from the collection, or the preference of one study room over another for group meetings.

Managers and leaders posses a particular ability to influence views of the organization held by staff members. The results we choose to communicate can orient staff members to act in different ways. Maybe our statistics are showing an increased use of the library website on Sundays. Communicating this to the reference staff may help them to staff online reference services appropriately over the weekends. Making staff members aware of this increase may cause other staff members to see opportunities unrecognized by managers. The increased use of the library site on Sundays may mean that announcements for upcoming events should be posted to the online events calendar on Sundays as opposed to Monday morning.

Libraries have been working at capturing knowledge and communicating it within the organization for decades. Many times this is done through informal, word-of-mouth channels. Sometimes we have tried the classic leave-a-note-book-at-the-reference-desk trick. Other times we have used the photocopier to run off the staff newsletter. These pre-web tools filtered information for organization members. Why do we care if technical services staff learn about the upcoming lecture series in the staff newsletter? Our egalitarian sentiments care because we know these staff members might want to attend the lectures. Our operations sentiments care because we hope that catalogers might recognize how items they are processing could complement the lectures and help connect the events to the resources.

Along these lines there are many news items within the organization that come up and go away before they can be communicated at formal meetings. This could be the need to alert staff members about the local VIP who just scheduled a visit to the library, the need for server maintenance over the weekend, or the temporarily amended scheduling to account for an individual who is sick. In all of these cases, the knowledge that is created either vanishes into the ether or risks being communicated unevenly across the organization.

Social media can act as real-time filters for information across the organization. They allow organizational members to capture ideas that flow past, sharing incidental knowledge as it comes up. This could be identifying immediate and obvious problems, such as "the exit to the back parking lot is closed today due to work being done on the doors." Or it could be not-so-obvious notes, such as "I just helped two students who only wanted photocopies of articles from printed periodicals, not from online databases or subscriptions." This may seem a bit out of the ordinary, but if three librarians each have students asking for the same thing, there is a reasonable chance that one of the teachers on campus is forbidding online sources. This might lead to contact from a librarian who might nicely ask the teacher to join the twenty-first century.

Social media make it possible to compensate for some of the looseness of the of library organization while highlighting its strength. As creative organizations, we need to have channels to capture our creativity and tighten up our lines of communication. Social media allow for the development of formal and informal sharing and documenting as never before.

Internal: collaboration

As loosely-coupled systems, library staff can organize and reorganize themselves to get work done. The marketing group meets, the social science bibliographers meet, and the cultural event planning group meets. When a new need arises, a new group can form to think about it. We want to be collaborative, and we want everyone have their input. Yet, sometimes we have the tendency to meet and meet and meet without actually getting any work done. We make the mistake in thinking that collaboration means talking and not working. A related problem is that collaboration essentially happens between people who actually work at the same time. Collaboration between the morning staff and the evening staff does not happen.

NEW YORK INSTITUTE OF TECHNOLOGY

Social media may help to alter some of this. Social media may not be the only answer to some of these challenges but they can foster an environment that might overcome them. A personality trait shared by almost all librarians is the desire to learn, and many libraries act as learning communities with people sharing, debating and engaging in issues around them. Knowledge sharing within the organization can strengthen this community, while disconnections between people weaken it. The more managers build connections between people, the more likely collaboration will occur.

Social media tools can be used as collaboration tools. They can be online work spaces allowing staff members to come together virtually. This could be synchronously or asynchronously. When we think about social media and collaboration, we have this idea of everyone gathered around their computers and looking at Facebook or another site. However, the real collaborative value for social media tools comes from the times between meetings. Social media tools can be used for "to do" lists, meeting notes or virtual documents.

A significant part of to making collaboration work is connecting and coordinating work. Social media can help make this happen. They may not be able to help us resist the urge to constantly hold committee meetings, but maybe they can help us be more productive between these meetings.

External: marketing and outreach

When we think about social media today, we often think about marketing and outreach to people outside of the library walls. In the not-so-distant past, libraries had a handful of options to spread the word about activities and services. We instituted newsletters to the community, and in extreme cases, some public libraries even purchased advertising on television. Of course, our funding has never supported much advertising, and we were at the mercy of local news outlets.

Clearly, the web has expanded the options and allowed libraries to directly communicate to patrons. Websites, email and now social media tools make it a bit easier to get our message out. The growth of library websites since 2000 has been exponential. The moves from HTML editing, to WYSIWYG editing, to social media have reduced the barriers for staff participation in the web world.

This presents challenges in terms of marketing and messages. In the pre-web world, managers and leaders could focus messages more easily, mostly because there were few outlets. Now, the challenge is that every staff member can access outlets. As new social medial tools come online, staff members set up their own fiefdoms to represent the library. Even worse, different staff members may set up different fiefdoms within the same site. The great thing with social media is that everyone can participate and take up the library's cause. The bad thing with social media is that everyone can participate and take up the library's cause. Managers and leaders need to recognize how to ensure that the library's message gets out in a somewhat coherent manner and that staff members are able to coordinate within and between particular tools.

Messaging is really one of the big challenges with marketing. It has been my experience that when libraries do communicate about new services, we are more likely just to report the existence of this service. We say things like, "hey, we have a new database." But we do not talk about why anyone would care or what people would do with that database like, "we can make business research easier for you with our new database." Social media tools do not make this challenge any easier. In fact, they may make it more difficult because all staff members must think from the user perspective.

As loosely-coupled systems, libraries benefit when more of their staff can easily participate in marketing and outreach. It can be tough for a single leader to identify the new and cool things happening within multiple departments. But marketing cannot be a free-for-all. There is a balance that needs to be achieved between the limits we felt pre-web and total anarchy.

Internal and external: giving your people a voice

Social media can give your people a voice, something that has internal and external implications. Social media can be a tool for empowerment by providing an avenue to shed light on unrecognized problems or by opening up conversations on issues in new ways. In 2006, *Time* magazine chose *you*—content creators on the web—for their annual person of the year issue (Grossman, 2006). They were making a statement about the distributed nature of the web in terms of content creation. In 2011, *Time* selected *protesters* as their person of the year, making a statement about the uprisings around the world, but also a statement about their tools (Anderson, 2011). The selection of *you* in 2006 seems a very muted and sedate contrast to *protesters* in 2011. 2006 makes me think about posting videos of cats to YouTube, while 2011 reminds me of revolutionaries in Tahrir Square in Egypt, rioting mobs in London, and the Occupy movement in the USA and elsewhere.

Obviously, protesting is not a new invention hatched by a web start-up out of somebody's garage. Yet, there is a new connectivity to today's protesters both within and beyond their movements. Social media tools have become coordination tools for these groups, helping them to arrange logistics. They have also become reporting tools, sending back immediate images and videos from the scene. Finally, they have also become advocacy tools for protestors to spread their message beyond the observers who happened to witness the protest and the journalists who decided to cover it, by connecting worldwide and giving justification and argument for their actions. In many ways, the physical protest has become an argument made to a virtual world. The face-to-face protest comes to an end, but its digital footprint goes forward.

Those of us within the library profession can easily forget that the concept of free information through a local library is a pretty radical concept and that individuals striving for social change use libraries or library-like approaches to hold up their efforts. For instance, the People's Library (*http:// peopleslibrary.wordpress.com/*) was at the heart of the Occupy Wall Street protests. As the occupiers formed their community, their library took shape to bring the community together, and when the New York Police Department evicted the protestors from Zuccotti Park, the library was destroyed (Moynihan 2012). Another less extreme example is the Read/Write Library in Chicago. This is a community-based, non-profit library that has an open acquisition mission. It accepts all donated materials in an effort to preserve and promote voices within the community. It operates through volunteers and donations (Velez, 2011). The Halifax Public Library in Canada presents another example of integrating community into library operations. Halifax transformed its services through a community-led approach which opened up planning to all members of the community including underserved populations (Williment et al., 2011).

I bring this up not because I envision libraries as hubs of social unrest, even though I am sure that our profession had more than its fair share of people in the streets. Rather, this illustrates the power of connecting people advocating for change. Our communities are full of these people. They are in civic groups, religious organizations, schools, non-profit organizations and political groups. Librarians should be careful how they enter into this area, but there is no doubt that we offer services and resources that would add value to these communities. For instance, this might involve doing a little research and writing up a blog post to support a local food pantry or maybe a post supporting fundraising at a nearby school. Librarians are active in their communities and are often in a position to recognize need and engage the community.

Giving librarians a voice online means to let them be themselves. Let librarians talk about their interests and let users connect online with people who they meet face-to-face. It is about empowering librarians to be people and not neutral observers of the world. This benefits the library by expanding its external reach. This should not be confused with marketing efforts. Marketing efforts may connect to this and offer context, but giving librarians and other staff members a voice goes beyond marketing. It is about growing ideas and connecting as individuals. The idea of a protester armed with social media as their weapon for change should be a model for librarians armed with social media as their weapon for connection. The ability to photograph, video and comment on the world needs to become our standard. The subject of posts could be "typical" library-related posts like new resources and new library spaces as well as posts about the community, such as the opening of new businesses, fundraisers for local schools, or cultural events offered by art clubs.

Storytelling is a powerful tool, and social media represent a way to extend our own stories. It need not be, "here's a photo of the pastries in our break room," but it could be, "here's a photo of the hardworking staff members who are processing new materials into our collection." This could include documenting remodeling, acquisition of new devices, and visits by local dignitaries. It could be about new staff members and longtime staff members. Our voice can be about how we accomplish our mission and the challenges we face in doing this under tight budgets and growing demands.

Of course, our story must also include the stories of our users. This could be stories about children receiving their first library cards, students doing research, genealogists working on local history, and gamers who come in to play in our tournaments. Our story may include the stories of the groups who use our meeting spaces or of the new art displays in our galleries. Our stories are the stories of our communities. We connect to the ups and the downs of our neighborhoods and our cities.

Internally, giving our people a voice means to open new avenues of communication across layers of our organizations. This may sound dangerous to some. It may be disruptive to some organizations. But, there is the potential to increase transparency across departments and vertically through the management structure. This could be about expressing concerns through internal blogs or pointing out problems that need to be addressed. Connecting via social networks, initiating discussions on blogs, or documenting work on wikis can create new channels for communication.

Giving voice to our people is related to the idea of capturing organizational knowledge, but it goes a step further. The challenge with loosely-coupled systems is that all members of the organization can be in a difficult position for judging success. In tight systems—especially for-profit systems—the measures of success are clearer. The ability to gauge whether things are going well can be more clearly observed, e.g. how quickly a product is created or how much revenue is generated. As loose systems, we have trouble evaluating our successes. This is even more difficult for managers who may not work directly with users. There is a difficulty in being close to the work and there can be many filters through which organizational success must pass. When managers can connect with staff and hear from staff, then issues can be expressed in a timely way and successes can be more apparent. Social media have the potential to flatten out the organization and connect in ways that might not otherwise be possible.

Internal and external: connecting virtual and physical

To many people, the "library" is still a building. To others, the "library" is a website where they go to access research databases or online journal articles. Our goal should be that the virtual complements the physical and vice versa.

In 2004, the first photos of the horrific tsunami that struck in the Indian Ocean did not come from the AP or Reuters. They came from cell phones in the hands of tourists who had witnessed the horror. Mobile technology has transformed all of us into first-hand reporters. Protests across the Middle East in 2011 have been aided by the ability to report back quickly without the filter of the news agency. I sometimes wonder if there is anything more powerful than a person whose mobile device has a camera and an internet connection.

The modern journalist is no longer just a writer who gets stories to editors by deadline. The modern journalist is a multimedia professional who tweets story notes, captures images, shoots video, and still writes the story by deadline. Imagine what we could do if we empowered our librarians to be more active in reporting their world or at least their libraries.

When librarians become the connectors of the physical and virtual, we can enhance both. This may mean that the virtual provides support and connections outward to happenings in the library (Figure 3.1). This could be by pulling in links to video, articles and other sources that expand displays,

Figure 3.1 Skokie Public Library using Facebook to connect to patrons

lectures or art exhibits. It might mean capturing audio or video of story times or book discussions. It might mean interviews with local authors or local government officials.

Our libraries gain internal and external benefits from connecting the virtual to the physical. Externally, we can open up the library to many people who may never come through our doors. This may include people unable to come to the library or may include people who are not aware of what we offer. Internally, this spreads awareness of our activities to all of our staff by connecting staff members who are separated by time and space. It also allows our staff members to connect a string of events over time and to preserve some of our work for the future.

Disintermediation

All new information technologies have the potential to shift the existing order. Five hundred years ago, the translation of the Bible from Latin into other languages paired with the printing press caused conflict at the time of the Reformation. Were church leaders *really* upset at people reading scripture in other languages? Perhaps they were they concerned that the translator might make mistakes? Of course not. The conflict arose out of the perceived threat to church authority. It arose through removing the priest as an intermediary to practicing religion.

As media scholar Clay Shirky has noted when comparing social media with the disruption caused by printing in the sixteenth and seventeenth centuries:

> As with the printing press, it doesn't take us from point A to point B. It takes us from point A to chaos. The printing press precipitated 200 years of chaos moving from a world where the Catholic church was the sort

of organizing political force to the Treaty of Westphalia where we finally knew what the new unit [for political organization] was, the nation state. (Shirky, 2005: 19:21)

Like printing, the rise of the internet has brought about different types of disintermediation. Postal services around the world struggle as revenues drop due to the replacement of letter writing with email (Rosenthal, 2011). The journalism industry has seen a significant reduction in force as budgets have crumbled due to the decline in advertising revenues and subscriptions (Hachten and Scotton, 2012). The music, publishing and film industries all feel their distribution and revenue streams shifting beneath them (Levine, 2011).

As librarians, we have felt this threat to our own existence as we are evolving our services from the print-based world to the fully-digital world. Even though librarians should be prepared to lead the way into disruptive technologies, many times they are not. It's not just that we fear what the print-to-digital shift means for us in terms of collections and how we do our jobs. I believe that it is just as much, or even more so, a fear of disintermediation. It is more often the change in power dynamics that causes us to be afraid.

As we push social media forward and as we see these tools as a way to connect people and be more visible in our communities, managers and leaders need to consider how prepared we are for the disruptions that will arise. When we ask librarians to blog about what they are actually seeing in the library, are we prepared for what this means? Is that what we really want them to do? Academics and activists may push for the transparent, open library where our problems are honestly communicated and we advocate for the needs of our users. In the abstract, I find this to be a seductive idea. In practice, however, it frightens me. The staff member with a bone to pick with administrators and a worldwide, information distribution platform should concern all of us. Twenty librarians blogging about anything and everything may sound good on the inside, but from the outside it may look like multiple personality disorder. Even worse, it may appear that the library has lost sight of its mission as community members wonder why tax money is being spent for librarians to commentate on everything under the sun.

Don't misunderstand. Libraries need to be more open and more engaged, but we also cannot afford to be naive. We have seen stories of universities suing students over blog posts and conflicts in the workplace arising from Facebook updates. Our libraries exist in the real world, which is a world impacted by social and political forces. Just as we can engage our communities in positive ways, we also can engage it in less fruitful ways. Disintermediation poses risks, so we must be prepared. If we expect librarians to really engage our community, we must create a context for this to happen in healthy ways that protect the organization and protect the individual.

We must also create a healthy context within the organization so that we do not distract ourselves from our goals. Internal conflicts can get in our way and undermine our efforts. Additionally, with limited time and resources, we can hardly afford to have our staff members stretched across platforms and working against each other. Disintermediation of one form or another is coming whether we like it or not. We must recognize the possibility that *we* might be the ones who get disintermediated if our libraries do not adapt and change in the evolving information world.

Leaders and managers must pull off a tricky balancing act. They need to work to tighten a loose system in order to capture knowledge and help draw connections between employees and departments. At the same time, they must avoid undermining the looseness that allows libraries to flex and change over time.

4

Defining a purpose

Abstract: Library managers and leaders can connect social media to the organization's mission by setting goals and providing a focus for organizational members. Managers need to consider how services are unfolded and how they will be adopted by organizational members. Many social media tools will be treated as gadgets that do not directly impact organizational goals. Defining a purpose around social media helps to directly tie the technology to the need. Libraries can join the larger conversations that are already happening in their communities. Social media can enhance connections to community groups, spread library-related news, and capture library-hosted events. Social media can also become the infrastructure for networked decision making, which overcomes the limits of past, top-down approaches to decisions.

Key words: social media, libraries, loosely-coupled systems, purpose of technology, technology adaptation, content curation, promoting events

Introduction

My wife does not like onions. This is one of the ongoing challenges in our relationship, but we have learned to deal with it. When we swing by a fast food restaurant for a burger, I have come to understand the challenge of ordering a cheese burger with no onions. Even though I enjoy onions quite a bit, I have learned that being married to a non-onion-eater means that the existence of onions can negatively impact my own meal. Thus, ensuring that onions are not placed on my wife's food becomes important. When ordering, it is important to repeat the request to remove onions from the sandwich at least twice. The first time should come immediately after requesting the cheeseburger. "I'd like a cheeseburger without onions." The second time should be at the end of the order right before paying: "Just wanted to check to be sure that you hold the onions on one cheeseburger." Then, before sitting down or before taking the food, it is important to check the specific cheeseburger to ensure that onions are not there. This strategy improves the odds of getting a personalized order in a fast food restaurant from around 50 percent to about 80 percent.

The reason for this is obvious to most of us. Fast food chains are highly standardized. They standardize their process in order to reduce mistakes by employees and to ensure food quality and appearance at thousands of establishments around the world. Of course, the problem faced by my wife—and me by extension—is that she does not enjoy this standardization and is in the difficult position of trying to force this system to do something different. We have concocted our own specialized approach to ordering so as to increase our odds of success. Of course, my personal strategy is to like onions, so my order is always right. However, I have learned not to suggest this strategy to my wife.

Any time a user accesses a service, a significant amount of the interaction will be predefined by how the service is offered. Were I to visit a tailor, get measured, pick out cloth, and describe what I want, the tailor could create a one-of-a-kind suit just for me. On the other hand, I could drive down to my local wholesaler, look through racks of identical suits and select the one that most closely matches my size and taste, even if none match perfectly. Most services can be considered on a continuum between highly personalized and highly standardized.

When a customer goes into a standardized service, the customer must learn how they will interact with the service. The individual who accesses a highly personalized service needs to know very little, because the service will adapt exactly to his or her needs. The individual who accesses a highly standardized service needs to understand how and to what degree the service can be manipulated to reach his or her needs.

The Starbucks chain of coffee shops is a fascinating example of balancing standardization and personalization. They have many, many options for changing their drinks. Each option is standardized, but there are so many options that it is difficult not to feel that one can order a one-of-a-kind creation, such as a half-decaf, grande, soy, mocha with a shot of vanilla. Their baristas manage the range of options by having a standard ordering process that roughly follows this outline: iced/non-iced, size, type of drink, and any special flavors to be added. If a customer orders coffee in the wrong order, the barista politely says the order back in the correct order as a friendly instruction for next time. I purposely order my drinks out of order just to see if they can handle it, "vanilla, skim (they don't use the word "skim" for anything), latte, grande." This drives them nuts.

My ordering like this results from my own mischievous nature, and I am probably guilty of enjoying the difficulty I cause people who are just doing their jobs. Of course, the point of this system for ordering coffee is to gain efficiency and limit mistakes. In order to do this, the system doesn't just train employees, but it also trains users. The reason the barista repeats the order back to me in the correct sequence is to influence my behavior so that I can order correctly next time. For some reason, I gain pleasure from pushing back a bit against this system.

There are lessons here for librarians. We too have a choice about the degree to which we standardize or personalize our services. Whether or not we know it, we think about this when we talk about the length of time librarians spend with a user at the reference desk. We also think about this when we create online guides, signage or information literacy sessions, all of which encourage users to be independent. Some days our librarians may be able to work with users for extended periods of time, giving them very individualized service. Other days, we are too busy, and librarians must perform triage in helping users, where we weigh needs and distribute our time. We always want our users to be independent so that they can access our services without our help. But this means that users must find ways to learn our systems and break through the layers of processes and rules we have in place. Ideally, we would give users very individualized service meeting their exact needs, but we know that this is not always possible.

When we think about social media and how we offer our services, we must think about how we unfold these services. How will we personalize our connections with our users, and, just as importantly, to what degree will we expect our librarians to act as individuals? We must decide whether we expect our social media services to be individual librarians connecting with individual users or whether these services will be a generic library voice broadcasting out to many users. There is a spectrum here in how we can break down our services. We can also think about how social media can work across our existing services to cut through some of our own standardization. We can use social media to connect in new ways that may allow us to step beyond our own walls, processes and ways of thinking.

Technology adoption

In *Megatrends*, John Naisbitt (1982) defines three broad phases for technology adoption within a culture. In the first phase, the new technology follows the path of least resistance. Users play around with it and try it out. I have also heard this called the gadget phase. The new technology is largely a novelty that shows potential, but has not really altered the way things are done. I remember signing up for the social networking site Hi5 back around 2005 or 2006. I signed up, created an account, and even invited a few of my friends to join. However, most of my close friends were not actively using social networking sites. They were definitely not on Hi5. After I signed up and made a page, I kind of sat there and wondered what I should do next. There wasn't much to do. I was about three to four years away from most of my friends and family posting every detail of their lives via social media. By that time, of course, they used Facebook and not Hi5. In 2005, social networking was definitely in the gadget phase for most of us. It was something to tinker with but not really something with a major impact on our lives.

In Naisbitt's second phase, users adopt technology as a replacement to improve things that they already do. In this phase, the technology makes life easier as it displaces older technologies. For instance, messaging in social media sites has largely replaced letter writing and even some volume of emailing. I remember feeling very empowered back in the early 1990s when I received my very first calling card. I could use any payphone to make a call, and the charges would be placed on my home phone account. Now, it is impossible to find a payphone. Cell phones have made public payphones obsolete along with my calling card.

In Naisbitt's third phase, the technology becomes transformative. The technology enables a whole new set of actions that could never have been done without it. Facebook has brought together email, chat and discussion boards, but it has taken these a step further. The ability to combine location data and to connect Facebook with external sites has made sharing seamless. They have enabled a degree of interactivity across the web that was not possible in the past. It's not that sharing didn't happen, but it couldn't happen like it does today.

As managers and leaders, we have to recognize that many technologies will exist in the gadget stage for a long time. Some will grow and move beyond it, but others will not. The gadget phase may sound unimportant, that it is something silly or childish. Leaders and managers overlook and undervalue the gadget phase. They often do not even recognize when it is occurring, and they rarely encourage it. But, the gadget phase can be very important. This is the time when new technologies gain attention and demonstrate potential. The seed is planted.

Over time, social media tools will come and go and many of them will never move beyond the gadget phase. For some tools, this is because their functionality may not align with staff needs. But for some tools, the functionality may be very useful, and staff may still avoid them. This is because really engaging users in social media requires librarians to move into the arena of ideas. Engaging users in the realm of ideas has inherent risks to employees such as entering controversial debates and potentially angering one side or the other. Most employees are savvy enough to avoid conflict and not risk workplace conflict. Therefore, they avoid truly developing many tools. They may tinker around with social media tools, but they do not really use them to actually engage users. They carefully steer clear of risk and keep the tools on a permanent back-burner. Confusion around the level of the service complicates this. Are librarians accessing social media tools as individuals or are they creating department-based accounts?

Organizational members need clarity around social media. While they do not need to be told exactly how to use each and every social media tool, they do need to have some context around the tools. Part of this context needs to address the level of service or the level of connection that the library will make via social tools. This may vary depending on the tool, but without guidance, most social media tools will be doomed to haunt the gadget phase forever. Managers and leaders must recognize that enabling action requires context and context requires a definition of purpose. *What is the value of social media tools for our organization?* Answering this question identifies our purpose.

The difference between marketing and community

The simple notion of liking something has become powerful. "Your friend likes this" grabs our attention because our friends often share similar interests. Naturally, this is a marketer's dream come true as users self-identify as liking a product, service, person, institution, article, video, etc. and then pass it along to their friends who may also connect with it. PR firms have long known that a significant portion of advertising revenue is wasted because it does not reach its intended audience. Newspaper and television advertising have been extremely inefficient because the only way to reach the small percentage of people who will use a product is to send the message out to everyone. Social media are changing this as users help to spread the word to their friends. Of course, marketers also know that nothing turns off users more than an inauthentic experience. Fake people and fake videos can cause a backlash. People do not like to feel like they are being duped or being played for a dupe. Marketing experts continue to seek out the elusive authentic experience. Connecting customers to products in authentic ways pays big dividends. Think about the success Apple has had in turning its products into something more than just technology tools. The company is marketing ideas around a lifestyle as much as it is marketing consumer electronics. PR experts are recasting marketing as an exchange between user and product, not as a one-way broadcast about a product (Lefebvre, 2007).

Libraries are better positioned to offer authentic experiences than most marketing firms, because we *are* authentic. We seek out actual needs and are not trying to sell anything. I have been to many marketing workshops for librarians where participants are given a big packet of marketing materials and told how to make a marketing plan. Now, I'm sure the people who run these workshops are very intelligent and I'm sure the information they present is really useful, but there are a few things that I never hear them say. I never hear them say that every contact made with the public is marketing. I never hear them say that the best marketing a library can have is the absolute greatest service. Instead, it is as if there's this unwritten belief that a library can market its way to success. The reality is that doing our job to our best abilities is the best marketing we have. Social media tools should be the tools that we use to do our jobs. They should be used to help our patrons reach their goals.

There is a difference between marketing and community. Marketing is communicating value in an effort to extend services, which is important to libraries. Community, on the other hand, is about engaging users and being part of their lives. Community is a give and take. It feels more like being a neighbor. This distinction should not escape libraries.

Apple has done a brilliant job of manufacturing community around its products, but for us there should be nothing to manufacture. The community is out there. We just need to consider how to make connections. Yes, libraries need to market themselves. But, the purpose around social media should be more than marketing. It is not possible to overstress the need for community.

The first step in defining purpose is to consider the value that social tools offer. This value can help us consider how standardized this service should be and how we can move tools past the gadget phase and toward more innovative uses.

Joining the conversation

The most compelling reason for libraries to engage in social media is to join the larger conversations happening around them. Drawing on our information resources is a significant way for this to happen. From their inception, librarians have played the role of information filter. Our essential role of collecting information for communities of people has remained unchanged for centuries, even as the ways we perform this task have dramatically shifted. Our society still has a need for us to be access points for information. This remains especially true as long as specialized content still has a cost attached to it (purchasing physical items, purchasing access to online tools, or supporting the infrastructure to access, such as internet access). This also remains true as long as significant portions of the population cannot afford to purchase their information.

In libraries, content should remain king. Social media can be utilized to maintain this focus as we can now show off and promote content as never before. This may take the form of book reviews, virtual book groups, connecting users to video or articles that enhance popular books, and many other avenues. We need to find the people who love reading, parents and students who need support, job seekers, community members who attend our events, activists working on local issues, neighbors of our branches, hobbyists using our resources and leaders of library friends groups. Every one of these groups is a potential audience for us to engage.

When it comes to joining the conversation, there is no better tool than a blog. Blogs allow for article-length pieces that are initially organized by date, but can also be categorized and shared. Blogs allow for thoughtful discussion around any topic, pulling in references to books in a collection, articles via databases, or embedded video from streaming services (Figure 4.1). This a great way to create and capture knowledge.

Figure 4.1 Video embedded in a blog

Another simple approach that could have a local impact is to set hashtags around local issues in Twitter. Hashtags operate like a subject label, pulling together tweets that share the same tag. This is a way to initiate a discussion on an issue by people who do not follow each other. It is a way to organize a larger conversation around an event. Twitter is great for live events like sporting events, political speeches, or protests where hashtags can be used to bring together real-time conversation. During the 2010 FIFA World Cup, there were country hashtags such as #arg, #mex, #fra, #eng and #nga. There was also a general World Cup tag which was simply #worldcup. Readers could follow conversation around one country or follow the larger conversation.

Hashtags have no rules and no central mechanism for approval or disapproval. They are simply created when someone types them. That's it. Hashtags come and go. They are like library subject headings that have broken free of our classification schemes. Tags are sloppy. Multiple tags refer to the same subject. They can be difficult to discover. On the other hand, they are easy to make. They are organic. They are extremely responsive. They tend to be used more when a recognized organization or individual connects a particular tag to an event, which is a perfect role for libraries. This could be as simple as using #LondonRdConstruction when tweeting about a local road improvement project or #headingtonschools when discussing local school issues. As a tweet can include links out to the web, this is a great way to share articles or links to a library blog for a more in-depth conversation.

A platform like Tumblr crosses the turf between a standard blog and Twitter. Compared with Twitter, Tumblr allows longer posts and embedding of content like audio and video. It also comes with a community of users who can easily share and move content. Tumblr is not as encompassing as a traditional blog like Wordpress for longer posts, but it is easy to implement and perfect for short posts. Tumblr could be great for quick content around projects that may include images or embedded video. Images from the local archives or even photos from your librarians' visit to a local museum would make great uses for Tumblr.

In all of these examples, the library staff member must be knowledgeable about the community and have content to contribute. For many staff members, the technical side of social media does not present the most significant challenge. Many staff members fear the actual content more than they fear the technology. Having something to say can take work and some risk. This requires stepping into the role of content creator. It also requires recognition that the purpose of social media is content generation.

Generated content vs curated content in a fact-checking world

A great deal of debate has been happening around the transformations occurring in journalism and the increased role of citizens as reporters in their own communities. The debate is important and warranted as local news outlets vanish into the night. Ironically, this technological shift is occurring as the information glut overwhelms us. As publishers and news media are disintermediated, writers of all stripes are pushing information online. Readers are left to fend for themselves against the onslaught. David Weinberger (2012) describes a crisis of knowledge as institutions and publishing structures that lend authority and credibility to information are undermined by the online world. Any opinion and crazy idea in the world can find support and "facts" somewhere on the web. The web has unleashed relativistic chaos where any idea is just as good as the next. The institutions that have supported public discourse over the years are being redefined and new institutions are being developed.

As a result, many news organizations have started to launch fact-checking services in an attempt to tame the avalanche of facts used in the political sphere. Sites such as the Fact Check Blog from Channel 4 News (*http://blogs. channel4.com/factcheck/*) in the UK and Politifact from the *Tampa Bay Times* in the USA, attempt to check the numbers and weigh in at times when political leaders bend data to meet their needs. Any regular citizen of the web knows that myth-busting sites like Snopes are essential to sorting through the bias and flat-out misinformation that proliferates on the web. Weinberger (2012) notes the irony that at the same time that the web makes information delivery effortless, the effort it takes to sort through the discourse makes the information unusable. We are living through a utopia and dystopia at the same time.

There is an opportunity here for libraries. We can be islands of order in a tumultuous sea. To some degree, journalism and libraries may walk down the same path as arbiters or brokers of information. Libraries can join the discussion by offering resources, discussing credibility, and acting as grounds for healthy debates. As noted in Chapter 1, filtering information is an important strategy for managing the information glut.

Ironically, filtering content by curating collections is what librarians have been known for over the last few centuries, but most local libraries have not engaged in online curation to a large extent. Social media may be an avenue to make this manageable. First, we have to consider that "curation" may not mean cataloging to MARC standards. It may mean organizing content in more temporary collections that are put together for short-term needs. It may also mean longer-term collections of digital content.

There are many organizations in local communities who have an interest and need for short and long-term content. Local historical societies, museums, religious organizations, schools and youth organizations can be supported through mini-collections. On college campuses, this might include academic departments, theater groups, student organizations, college initiatives or college administrators. In all cases, collections of sources, annotations of sources, or longer write-ups can give context and support for activities. This may be as simple as posting a single link on Facebook in support of a new college initiative or posting a link with additional information on an exhibit at a local museum. This also could be more in-depth collections that require formal organization and explanation.

Curation activities can go beyond simple distribution of links for local organizations. Many of these groups have their own content to contribute but do not have the infrastructure to make this possible. The local historical museum may have digital images or documents that can be digitized and shared. These could be uploaded, annotated, shared via the web and even organized with metadata. Groups in the community have a great deal of content to contribute if the library has ways to seek this out. Library leaders must consider whether librarians or staff members will gather and upload content or if community members will contribute content themselves. Curated content may be organized and posted using a social bookmarking tool like Delicious or shared via sites like Reddit or Stumbleupon that aim less for long-term access of information.

Part of the value that libraries can add for these community groups is establishing credibility, recognition and awareness. Naturally, as curation projects move forward, we must recognize that what is *not* collected is as important as what *is* collected. Care must be exercised as librarians determine the length of projects and the level of ongoing support that the library will provide. Social media and the web provide many options for making content accessible to the public. Some options are inexpensive and easily utilized by lone individuals. Other options require more technological support and planning.

In the past, information creation and distribution was expensive, so libraries remained in the collection business and out of the creation business. As physical media have given way to digital, the lines between creation, collection, distribution and storage have blurred. Just as journalism is moving toward hyperlocal and citizen journalists to collect and curate content, libraries have similar opportunities as we recognize that content is not something that comes from publishers, but is something created all around us.

News about the library

One clear-cut and very useful purpose for social media is spreading news about a library's services, events, facilities and staff. Most libraries are engaging in this via email, social networking pages, blogs and information on their websites. As local newspapers have cut pages or folded altogether, libraries have been spreading their message using the effectiveness of the web. With social media, it is easy to make a fairly attractive page.

With the rapid spread of social media, managers and leaders must recognize that all library staff have a role to play in disseminating information about the library. Our organizations are very active, and members in each department may produce "news" that they want to get out to users. There is the potential of a cacophony of library voices clogging Facebook pages or posting to blogs. Ironically, in many libraries, the posting of news falls to one, lone voice, often the poor person who started up the library blog. This person must know about and understand the significance of newsworthy items and then have the time and energy to write up posts. The advantage of libraries' loosely-coupled nature is missed. (Chapter 5 deals with these challenges.)

A question facing managers and leaders is whether the library has an official news channel or whether librarians and staff members are free to publish news. Do department heads, professional staff, or others need approval from supervisors? Does news need to be filtered and checked for accuracy before it is published, and what kind of delay does this review put on the publication of news?

On my campus, our library is fairly free to use our blogs, campus email and other social networking tools to spread news about the library. The college also has a public relations department that acts as the "official" voice of the college. I can submit draft press releases or just details about events and services. The PR staff members review my submissions and weigh them against the larger needs of the school. Most of the time, my submissions make the cut and are distributed. Nevertheless, there are times when my information may not be included. When that happens, I rely on my library's social media tools to spread the word. I know that local news outlets (online and in print) and other local groups who share information pay more attention when my information comes directly through the campus PR office, which manages the college's main Facebook and Twitter accounts and have more followers than my library's social media pages. Depending on the size of the library, leaders and managers may want to consider the role of department pages versus a library-wide page. Does the library need a way to decide what counts as news?

Capturing events

As discussed in Chapter 3, social media's impact has been greatly felt by protesters and activists. For them, protests have become as much for online consumption as they are for the actual time and place. They are using social media to extend protests into the virtual world, giving them a life that carries forward beyond their temporal existence. Libraries can learn from this. The promotion of cultural events and programming offered by libraries definitely falls into the news category, but capturing these events and moving to the online world is something different.

Lectures, children's programs, art displays, book talks and other events can get additional exposure and life through the web. As discussed, the most basic and perhaps essential way that social media can support programming is through promotion. Blog posts, tweets and Facebook posts should be basic operating procedures in promotion.

Social media can easily enhance events with online support. This could include short written pieces that link to books, articles or other information sources. These may include artist statements for art exhibits or historical notes to add context to musical performances. It may include the incorporation of location-based tools such as Foursquare to spread the word about events as they happen.

People love images. The use of images online has become increasingly easier as cameras on mobile devices have improved and the costs of digital cameras have come down. Uploading images to Flickr or creating albums on Facebook is pretty easy. Sending out images after the fact is a way to capture some of the event as documentation to show that libraries are doing their jobs. Images are also a way to remind people who were there about the success of the program and to show off the event to people who did not attend. It is a way to say, "we do these kind of events, so keep an eye out for more in the future."

Another enhancement for cultural events is the use of hashtags in Twitter. This is a great way to encourage the audience to engage with live events in virtual space. Audience members who do not know each other can use the same hashtag and comment and hold an online discussion in real time. I have been to many conferences where the organizers predefine the hashtag and participants then tweet notes and images from presentations. This is great way to have audience members filter information as it happens. I have to admit that I have followed many conferences from my office via Twitter, because I could not spend the money or time to attend. Hashtags can turn anonymous audience members into a valuable part of the event.

Along these same lines, Twitter can be used to bring people together as a "Tweetup." This is a meet up of people who tweet around a topic. It turns the physical world into a complement of the virtual world. Tweetups tend to be more successful in instances where people care deeply about a topic and have a rich, online discussion. Rich online discussions bring people together to have rich face-to-face discussions, and, of course, additional tweets about the Tweetup. Libraries can organize Tweetups and encourage these events.

When it comes to extending an event into the virtual world, images of events and supporting information about events add value, but they are not quite the same as the event. Social media present opportunities to distribute the event itself. The most straightforward would be videos of events posted to YouTube or distributed as a video podcast (Figure 4.2). Video does not replace the actual event, but video does allow discussions, lectures and presentations to be captured and shared. For nearly a decade, blogs have been used to "live blog" events. This means that a

Figure 4.2 Podcasts in iTunes

predesignated person types out notes about an event as it happens. Before bandwidths grew and before streaming video was common, live blogging was the best option for real-time, online broadcasting of events. Libraries can still do this very easily and inexpensively.

Video files can be large. They require a bit more knowledge in terms of recording, editing, storing and uploading. If video feels a bit out of reach, audio may be more manageable. There are many affordable MP3 recorders that can be used to record discussions. The MP3 file format has proven to be very versatile. MP3 files can be linked to in blog posts, they can be uploaded with a static image to YouTube, and they can be turned into a podcast for distribution in iTunes. Free audio editing software like Audacity allows for the editing of files. The audio of an event misses the visual elements, but audio is easy to manage and captures the key content for most events. Audio matched with a PowerPoint presentation can be quite effective.

A step beyond capturing events would be organizing fully virtual events. Large-scale live events can be difficult, requiring a streaming server and technical know-how. However, there are many more accessible options. Skype can be utilized to bring together individuals for an interview that is recorded for later distribution. Google Voice or Audacity can be used to record phone conversations that can be turned into a podcast or online recording.

In some ways, cultural events and programming are low-hanging fruit for libraries. They represent valuable content and information sharing. Events engage the community and bring people together to share ideas. Events turn the library into a public learning space where discussion and sharing thrive. Most libraries already host events, and social media can be used to extend the events and broaden their impact.

User contributions

The possibility of libraries curating content from community organizations is discussed above, but this can be taken further. Talented individuals across our communities have contributions to make. Guest bloggers such as local political leaders, local educators and local religious leaders could write about issues and activities in the area. Librarians could invite original contributions from leaders, or they could keep an eye out for exciting pieces published in community newsletters or local blogs. With permission, existing content can sometimes be "repurposed."

Crowdsourcing has become a popular idea on the web. Crowdsourcing uses the web to distribute work among many people, each of whom contribute a small portion of the work. This enables the crowd to accomplish tasks that would take individuals a prohibitive amount of time. In the UK, *The Guardian* famously initiated a crowdsourcing project when it recruited the public to help review nearly

500 000 pages of MPs' expenses claims to examine how MPs were using public money. Libraries may want to avoid divisive political debates, but they could take on other projects such as posting old photos to Facebook and asking users to identify individuals.

Many integrated library systems are following Amazon's lead by allowing users to write reviews of books and other resources in library collections. The local tool for this kind of work is a reader blog where users submit reviews about their favorite books. Book group members can offer write-ups before the book groups meet. Readers are lovers of ideas and often looking to find others who love their favorite authors and characters. Virtual book groups can be organized in social networking sites such as Ning where individuals can post to their own blogs but also share on discussion boards. Facebook pages can be created for particular authors or particular themes. Users can help to curate links, but they can also contribute their own, original ideas.

Capturing internal knowledge

Several years ago, one of our librarians at our reference desk received a call from a college staff member asking about Public Law 195. They told us that this law required our students to pass a test on the Illinois State Constitution (where my college is located). There was a reference to Public Law 195 in college documents, but college staff could not find the law or any additional information. A Google search revealed that other colleges in our area also reference Public Law 195. After a great deal of research, including several phone calls to government agencies, our librarian learned that there was no such thing as "public law." We had "public acts," but there was no Public Act 195.

We didn't know where Public Act 195 originated, but it did not refer to anything legally binding. Our librarian did find reference to requirements for students in lower grades taking a test on the Illinois Constitution, but nothing clearly about requirements that might impact our students. This research took many days to track down and confirm from individuals in the state. In an effort to document this work, our librarian posted it to one of our library's blogs (Public Law 195, *http://ext.morainevalley.edu/searchtips/?p=313*). For many years, this blog post was the first result returned by Google when one searched for "public law 195" (at the time of writing, the post was at number 6). The post was also shared via email among our local colleges.

This post about Public Act 195 is a classic example of useful information being created, captured and shared on a blog. As discussed in Chapter 3, an advantage that social media offer to our libraries as loosely-coupled systems is the ability to capture and share internal information. A reference blog is definitely a perfect tool for showing off searches, reviewing new resources and pointing out search tips to users. More concise posts could be made to Facebook, Twitter, Google+, Tumblr and many other platforms. Information services, reference advice and the identification of useful tools remain at the heart of what we do, and we should take every opportunity to show them off—not only are there marketing benefits, but this makes our services carry on long after the interaction has ended.

Beyond reference, social media present ways for staff to stockpile organizational knowledge. Wikis are extremely useful for organizing and editing policies and procedures online. Wikis can be hidden behind a password so that they are not open to the public. They are easily edited so that they can be updated over time. The fact that they live online means there is no worry about which version is current or where the file is located on someone's hard drive. Additionally, formal policies can be given context by being placed next to guidelines, best practices or a bit of history. In addition to wikis, policies and guidelines can also be shared using a social, document-sharing site like Scribd. This is a site where documents, images and other files can be uploaded and described. The files can easily be embedded in other sites or just linked up. Scribd preserves the actual document as it was formatted. Viewers can comment on files or share them.

This is similar to Slideshare, which hosts slides in PowerPoint, PDF and similar slide formats. Slideshare can be a nice option for spreading the word through images and text. The progression of slides can be an effective way to build an argument for staff members or members of the public who do not have time to sit and read newsletters or emails. Both Scribd and Slideshare allow others to embed outside information in their sites.

Collaboration

As mentioned in Chapter 3, social media can bring staff members together to get work done. Collaboration can go beyond emailing documents toward a more efficient effort. As mentioned above, staff wikis allow for the sharing of ideas and information. This could be meeting notes summaries and "to do" lists. Facebook provides private group pages that can be accessed only by designated individuals. With Facebook's browser version on desktops and app version on mobile devices, this can be an easy to use way to share notes and update individuals on the progress of projects. A social site like Ning can also allow staff members to share ideas and schedule events easily.

Our library has maintained a staff forum blog as a way to share information between our library staff members. This works as a makeshift staff newsletter. It is password protected so that it is not open for the whole world to read. The advantage of the blog for us is that it is easy to identify new information as new posts appear at the top. We can set up email alerts so that staff members are alerted to new posts. The blog is searchable so posts can be found more easily than if they were just email announcements. Additionally, other staff members can leave comments and help to contribute to ideas. The staff forum blog is not direct collaboration between staff members. However, it is an avenue to share information easily so that innovations and changes in the environment can be quickly disseminated. It is an important step toward creating an innovative environment.

As will be discussed in Chapter 5, coordination relies on communication. Individuals must be able to access sites and make decisions about what work needs to be done. They must then be able to submit their work for the benefit of others. Communication is the lifeblood of collaboration. Creating an infrastructure for communication is a first step toward enabling cultural change in the organization. As we will see, creating the infrastructure does not necessarily change the culture. But without the infrastructure, change will be slowed.

Decision making

In 2004, James Surowiecki seduced armchair organizational theorists with *The Wisdom of Crowds*, where he demonstrated ways that groups of people can make better decisions than any individual in that group. He emphasized the value of prediction markets, which operate like stock markets and are used to predict the outcomes to questions. The leading example of a functioning prediction market is InTrade, where individuals can use actual money to purchase stocks related to real-world events. Political observers often visit InTrade to check the predicted outcomes of elections. Another prediction market is the Hollywood Stock Exchange (*www.hsx.com*), where users help to predict the success of a film from its inception through its eventual release in theaters. Surowiecki's work outlines the ways that individuals can come together to make decisions. Sadly, although his arguments are persuasive, his approaches (notably the prediction markets) are beyond the reach of most organizations, including most libraries. Some online polling is the best that most libraries can offer.

Weinberger's (2012) approach to decision making moves toward more practical application. In the title of his 2012 book, he tells us that information on almost any topic is *Too Big to Know* for any individual. There are—and always have been—too many pieces of information on almost all topics. The torrent of information on the web has made this more than apparent. A searcher can find information to support and refute any opinion or proposition. This is one of the reasons that Weinberger argues that the top-down, pyramid structure of most organizations is giving way to a networked decision-making structure. In a pyramid structure, knowledge is necessarily reduced as it moves up through the layers of management. There is too much information on any one topic to communicate all of it to leaders. Each level of management reduces details until the decision-maker at the top is left with abstractions and guesses. If middle managers edit out useful solutions, then the top of the pyramid cannot select them. Additionally, individuals across the organization have difficulties in communicating because communication occurs up and down the organizational chart and not across. Innovations must travel up the pyramid; the leaders at the top must recognize how innovations may meet the needs of those below them, and act to implement the innovation. Innovations must flow up and then back down.

Weinberger assumes that no single individual can know enough, so leaders must rely on their networks, including their networked organizations. Knowledge is embodied by a network. Leadership becomes a process where people with useful knowledge come forward at the right time. The knowledge is matched with the situation. Leadership is less about the leader and more about the group being led. The group must be able to store and communicate information in order to make decisions.

This view of decision making matches a loosely-coupled system very well. In loose systems, like libraries, knowledge exists in pockets and leaders can draw on these pockets strategically. To make this happen, people within the network must be aware of problems in need of solutions, and leaders must be able to receive messages about potential solutions. Mechanisms for communication must be in place and organizational members must participate. This is an ideal role for social media because they can create a decentralized, two-way environment that does not sacrifice details and on-the-ground needs of departments. Social media also enable communication across organizational structures. This is related to the idea of capturing internal knowledge discussed in the section above, but the focus here is on how decision makers at all levels of the organization think about using knowledge to enact change.

Part of this decision-making potential arises out of the ability of decision makers to gain a broader view of the organization via social media. If leaders engage in social media to hold an ongoing dialog with organizational members, then they can gain broader perspectives. Online forums such as Ning, Google/Yahoo groups, private Facebook group pages, passworded wikis or blogs can be places where leaders can post ideas and ask organizational members to comment. Naturally, the environment and organizational culture must be utilized to encourage openness and sharing. Managers may be able to learn about activities within the organization via blog posts, tweets and Facebook updates.

The primary way that most employees learn about the organization is through word-of-mouth chatter. The primary technological avenue is through broad email blasts to multiple staff members. Neither of these methods allow leaders to capture and organize communications. Gossip channels are inaccurate and inefficient. Email blasts can be very efficient as a one-to-many stream of information, but they are an inefficient and wasteful mechanism for many-to-many. Social media offer mechanisms that can enable more efficient online group sharing.

Decision making in a social media enriched environment does not mean that everyone gets to make the decision or that that organizations must employ some complicated voting system. It primarily means that open communication channels exist, as does the ability for organizational members to offer solutions. It also means that managers can reorient the attention of the organization more efficiently. Managers and leaders can utilize social media to highlight problems and direct attention. They can also highlight and share successes. Management and leadership are a process of focusing attention and enabling action. Social media can be the infrastructure to make this happen.

Visibility

It may seem obvious that one outcome of social media is to increase a library's visibility, but it may be less obvious that visibility can bring about more visibility. When I was a new librarian, I convinced our director that we should be holding public events. This is something that our academic library had not really done in a serious way. After some discussion, she said yes, and we moved forward. We had some early bumps along the way. We needed to move around furniture, work with our campus multimedia services to set up a sound system, and then convince faculty members to speak in the middle of an open, active library. Our first events were poorly attended. But over time, we learned from our mistakes, reorganized our space, installed a sound system, and started podcasting events. At first, I spent several years begging faculty members to participate, but as we held more events, awareness grew. Event planners around campus recognized the advantage of being in an active space and having events distributed as a podcast. Over time, event organizers increasingly sought out the library as event space, and today, we organize a few of our own programs, but mostly events come to us (Figure 4.3).

Figure 4.3 Buddhist monks creating a sand Mandala in the Moraine Valley Community College Library

The more visible a library is, the more visible it will become. This isn't just true with public events and podcasting. Social media tools have a multiplier effect. As more people connect with a library, the more likely they are to share posts by its staff and the more likely they are to help increase the awareness around the library's content. A library's network does the work for it. But visibility extends itself beyond the virtual space. The online connects to the physical. As discussed earlier, the virtual extends itself into the physical in terms of marketing, user-generated content, and even jumping into important conversation. These are ways to extend visibility. We can target our actions to purposefully connect the physical and virtual. When we write online about local events and groups, we can encourage them to share what we have written. When we meet community leaders, we can even ask them to connect with us and with the library online. Naturally, the larger goal is that social media can help us demonstrate that our library is more than just a library—it is people too.

Finding a focus

Single social media tools such as Facebook, Twitter and blogs can serve many purposes unto themselves. This chapter has outlined options and presented a challenge around how tools work best with our goals. Managers and leaders face the difficult task of selecting a focus and encouraging participation. In loosely-coupled systems, allowing looseness around technologies can be an advantage. This allows experimentation. Managers do not need to understand exactly how a technology *should* be implemented at the outset. Organizational members can try out options and provide feedback. But managers must also be aware that most staff members work to avoid conflict. If they have a good head on their shoulders, they are cautious by nature. They keep an eye out for organizational landmines. As discussed in Chapter 2, organizational members also rely on a degree of predictability in their jobs. They rely on organizational control mechanisms to give them an outline of how the organization operates. Therefore, organizational members have a need for focus and context around new technology tools.

Managers should ensure a degree of looseness around tools, but they also must recognize that providing some definition around how technologies can be used will push innovation further down Naisbitt's phases of development. When new technologies arrive, people often understand new tools based on past technologies. This is why we have repurposed paper terminology for the online world in web *pages*, *folders* and *desktops*. In another example, the word *blog* is a simplification of *web log*. A log of course refers to a systematic recording tool, which dates back to the wooden floats used by ships on long voyages. We understand technologies based on what we know. We use technology to accomplish tasks that we already do, and we evolve new ways of thinking around the technology.

Chapter 5 examines how we can rethink organizational structures to enable adaptation and innovation around social media. But before this can happen, managers and leaders must consider the range of purposes that are possible. As library staff members have experimented with social media, they have undoubtedly uncovered many possibilities. Organizational staff members have experimented and dabbled with social media in their personal lives. Even if they are not information producers, most of them are social media consumers. Therefore, knowledge and experience already exist in the organization.

As discussed at the outset of this chapter, one question for managers and leaders to consider is the level of individualized service that a library will provide via social networking. Does each librarian, each department, or just the library as a whole have a Facebook page, blog or Twitter account? These are questions that members of the organization can help answer. Managers can employ a process to define a purpose and direction for action.

A first step is to identify what social media tools have been used within the organization. Managers and leaders probably have an awareness of some of the tools, but a more formal survey may be necessary to ensure that all tools are uncovered. The survey can try to differentiate between tools that are used professionally and personally. If the survey results show that staff members' knowledge of social media tools needs some enhancement, the library may want to consider following one of the versions of the "23 Things" discussions—a learning 2.0 program designed by Helene Blowers, Technology Director of the Public Library of Charlotte and Mecklenburg County, that has spread to libraries around the world. The 23 Things discussion is a great way to foster change in a library.

When managers highlight successful uses of specific technologies, they are sending the signal that this is something for others to replicate. Managers can send signals through awards, recognitions, mentions at meetings or write-ups in newsletters. There are many times when highlighting the technology is enough of an endorsement that others feel empowered to experiment. All the focus that is needed is a pat on the back. Of course, there will be times that more formal guidelines or policies need to be written. This may draw from a purpose or mission statement created for social media efforts. A purpose statement needs to address the two questions introduced way back in Chapter 1:

how will a particular tool be useful for me and *what information will I choose to share?*

When trying to define a purpose, managers should try to aggregate the views of a broad number of staff members. Getting people to think independently is important so that each person is not overly influenced by the most vocal or those further up the organizational chart. This can be done through a basic visioning exercise where staff members picture a perfect world. In the ideal world, how can social media address the needs of our users? Ask people to write out their views. Then, ask them to write out key ideas and post them on a wall or white board in a meeting room. Ask them to organize them as they post them. Organize ideas into tools, uses, goals, populations or any other categories that make sense. This exercise can be done in an afternoon as a group or over weeks individually. After participants have contributed, the exercise organizer can summarize the ideas and write them up into a workable document for comment and additional review. This is an iterative process where ideas are contributed and refined. This is most useful when the organization needs a push. The goal of discussions around social media should be not only to produce a statement or some written document, but also to create awareness, knowledge and ultimately action. People in the organization can identify ways that social media can improve services. They recognize a need. Sometimes, they may not know that they know. Managers can start a process to identify needs.

Start a good blog

Libraries that have not dabbled in social media may wonder where they should start. The answer may sound straight out of 2004, but it remains true: start a good blog. Blogs remain the most flexible social media tool. They allow for article-length posts, short posts, uploaded photos, embedded video and links to other pages. As discussed in Chapter 6, RSS can be used to redirect blog content to standard websites, social networking sites and mobile devices.

Additionally, blogs have low technological barriers. Anyone who can sign up for a free email account on Yahoo or Gmail can create a blog. Multiple staff members can post content, and they can use categories to add a layer of organization and searchability. For libraries that cannot afford full-blown content management systems, blogs can fill the role. The smallest library, tucked away in the most out-of-the-way hamlet can start a blog for free. Blogger and Wordpress remain the leading free, web-based blog platforms. Their broad user communities enable a great deal of online support.

Challenges of participation

Libraries face a few challenges in utilizing the social media world. Several revolve around encouraging our organizations to coordinate their work effectively, which is the focus of Chapter 5. But one challenge comes from users. Specifically, most do not access social media because they want to connect with libraries. Research shows that most users join tools like Facebook and Google+ in order to connect to people they already know (Smith, 2011). Most library Facebook pages have zero interactions from users (Gerolimos, 2011). Individual libraries will not be able to change these user habits overnight, but these habits can change. A decade ago, users would have never thought to email libraries or chat online with librarians, but today such interactions are commonplace. My library receives more emails, chats and texts from users than we do phone calls. Connecting via social media can follow this trend. Part of our efforts must focus on changing the expectations of our users.

Users expect us to be what we've always been: storehouses for information. Obviously, this is a role we do and should and continue to play. However, we should also continue to play our other role, which is a center of community. Our services are evolving within an ever-changing information world. As we consider how we can utilize social media, we must keep our larger goals in mind. The focus of social media must move our larger goals forward and make us more vital to the communities we serve.

Often, libraries have had standardized services limited by space, resources and our inability to reach beyond our library walls. Social media can help us break out of our own fast food tendencies. For decades, we have expected users to adjust to us, navigating our call number and subject headings. Part of our challenge was in our inability to reach out and connect. While we may not always be able to transform all of our services, we are now more able to share knowledge and connect to users.

5

Connecting social media tools to the organization

Abstract: Managers and leaders can embed social media into the fabric of the organization by using the four coordination tools: policies, budgets, organizational policy and participation rules. However, when these tools are implemented, managers face a conundrum of control: the more controls that are put in place around social media, the less useful the tools become. Nevertheless, managers must still work to coordinate their use as the misuse of social media can damage the larger organization. Policies are the foundation for setting the view of organizational members toward social media; budgets set the foundations for technology and training; organizational culture fills in the gaps; and participation rules define how staff members make decisions. Managers can define structures around social media to give coordination tools form and encourage staff members to participate. Managers and leaders must work to encourage employees to use tools and be ready to give appropriate attention to any complaints around social media.

Key words: collaboration, coordination, social media, Facebook, Twitter, Pinterest, Hootsuite coordination tools, policies, budgets, organizational culture, participation rules, complaints

Introduction

Imagine the staff of a library all sitting together in a large conference room. They are given the following options. If everyone in the room writes down the word "yes" on a piece of paper, then everyone gets a seven-day paid holiday. If even one person writes down "no," then the people who wrote down "yes" give up seven days out of their yearly holiday schedule. Anyone who writes down "no," gains and loses nothing. Staff members are not allowed to speak to each other as they decide what to write. If everyone writes "yes," then everyone benefits. If even one person backs out, those who took the risk suffer.

What would happen if this was actually tried with library staff? More than likely, staff members would look around the room and consider the trustworthiness of the other people sitting near them. They would think to themselves, "do I really think that each one of these people will write yes?" The odds would predict that at least one person would write "no." They would probably not be willing to take the chance. They would rather walk away without losing what they already had.

Now, imagine the same scenario. But, this time managers allow staff to talk to each other. What would be different? A stronger chance exists that peer pressure can change this outcome. The most vocal staff members could walk around and encourage everyone to write "yes." It may require answer checks and stern looks, but simple communication can change the outcome. Communication can build trust in the group so that all work together.

This example is a classic coordination problem. Behavioral economists and mathematicians who study game theory specialize in solving these types of problems. The heart of coordination problems is the need to trust and communicate.

In the first example, when staff members couldn't communicate, they struggle to trust each other. They know that at least one person will fail to participate. When communication occurs, it becomes easier for everyone to coordinate their actions.

As discussed in Chapter 2, coordinating action is a central challenge for libraries. As loosely-coupled systems, the service interactions offered by staff members are not directly tied to each other. We work in systems that create new knowledge as they interact with the world, but we often lose that knowledge immediately after it is created. This knowledge may exist in the heads of the people who created it, but in order for the system to benefit from it, the individuals must have sufficient recall to use it again. If other staff members are to benefit from the knowledge, they must know to ask about it. In Chapter 3 and Chapter 4, the ability to capture knowledge and join conversations was presented as an advantage of social media in loose systems. As many staff members will never work together, sharing across our social media infrastructure makes knowledge usable in new situations by multiple individuals.

But, as one can imagine, if staff members choose not to share, then social media provide no benefit for the organization. Social media can be likened to a party. The host can decorate and prepare food and drinks, but if no one shows up, it isn't a party. If only two people show up, then there will be some awkward conversation and uncomfortable silence. The challenge around effective social media implementation is getting library staff to see social media as an integral part of their jobs so that they choose to participate. If people are fearful of participation or do not see the value, they will not participate.

Decision making in a networked environment relies on the ability to access needed knowledge in context. Networked decision making is enabled by communicating across the organization. In traditional organizational structures, leaders and managers require knowledge to be filtered up the chain of command. Knowledge about the organization comes from observation, written documents and usage data, all of which can be disconnected from the actual interactions and services provided by the library. The challenge with traditional organizational structures is that they put pressure on managers to actually manage the structure and build mechanisms for data sharing. It is up to managers to share knowledge and connect individuals to each other. Social media can ease the pressure on managers to catch and aggregate all knowledge. Coordination thrives in environments where communication occurs easily and freely.

Not too long ago, before everyone had cell phones in their pockets, meeting friends at the local shopping mall required work to be sure you arrived at the same spot at the same time as your friends. Phone conversations were geographically bound from home to home. Once someone left his or her home, that person could not be reached unless he or she found a pay phone and tried to call home. If you were going to meet a friend or family member, locations and times for meeting needed to be set in advance. Today, coordinating trips with friends is much easier. As long as the parties involved select the same day or afternoon, they just need to make a quick call to find each other. We do not need to select a meeting point prior to arrival.

When members of the organization can coordinate their actions, there is less pressure on managers to predict the future because they can share problems more easily and access the knowledge of organizational members more easily. For this to work, managers and leaders must connect goals to the coordination tools—policies, budgets, organizational culture and participation rules—that turn a group of individuals into a functional organization. Yet, managers face a conundrum because the tools that help to coordinate individuals can also be the tools that limit the usefulness of social media.

Conundrum of control

The advantage of the loosely-coupled nature of libraries is their ability to create decentralized knowledge and share it across the organization. Departments and individuals can act as pockets of innovation, driving change across the organization simply by creating solutions for their own localized problems. This occurs when the localized solutions are shared and adapted across departments. In order for this to work, staff members must be able to experiment with new technologies freely. For example, a technical services department may want to examine its workflow in an effort to improve efficiency. The staff may decide to use Tumblr to document each step in their acquisitions and cataloging process. Other departments within the library may find this to be very useful, and library users may find this fascinating as it may give a face to an otherwise faceless process. The use of Tumblr as a documentation tool could become a novel idea within the organization and may lead to similar uses by other departments. In order for this to happen, the technical services staff members must know about and understand Tumblr, but they also must feel that this is an appropriate use of technology within the organization. If staff members were required to go through a lengthy approval process for a new blog on Tumblr, they may decide it is not worth the trouble, and potential innovations may be squashed before they have been tried out.

Individuals are more likely to discover innovations in open environments where they are free to play around with tools. Adaptability—literally the ability to adapt—increases in looser systems where coordination tools like policies, budgets, participation rules and organization culture do not hamper experimentation. As discussed in Chapter 2, coordination tools create a framework within which the organization exists by allowing individuals to come together, divide labor and get work done. But coordination tools also provide a degree of protection for organization members and for the organization itself. These tools define what is allowable and what is not. Often, formal policies define "right" and "wrong," and organizational culture fills in the gaps. So, if the technical services department wants to use Tumblr to document its cataloging process, the library's coordination tools will define whether or not this is permissible. Should the cataloging process be communicated outward to the public? Only the values and beliefs of a particular library can answer that question. In my own library, that would be no problem, but in other places, it may be frowned upon.

Thus, library managers and leaders face what Harvard University's David Weinberger (2007) calls a conundrum of control. This conundrum states that organizations need to utilize coordination tools in an effort to give form and offer control of tasks, messages and the actions of employees. But the more controls that are in place around social media, the less useful the tools become. The point of coordination tools is to provide definition, but definition is applied around technological applications that are already known. This means that new applications must be excluded or organizational members must seek approval for new applications, which can be cumbersome.

For example, a librarian may want to live blog a panel discussion that will be held in the library. Live blogging the event will allow real-time notes to be sent out as the event happens, but maybe no one has ever live blogged an event in the library. Maybe the library's blog has just been used for announcements and book reviews. What should the librarian do? The librarian could seek approval from supervisors, which may take meetings and documentation. The supervisor may need to take this idea to his or her supervisor. Managers may require a written description of live blogging, which may need to be included in the technology policy so that it is clear that this use is permissible. There is a point where the librarian will decide that the work to get this approved is not worth the effort. In smaller libraries, the layers of red tape may be easier to navigate, but the interpersonal dynamics may be just as cumbersome. If the library's blog has only been used for book reviews and news updates, then other staff members may think that live blogging an event is not an appropriate use of the technology. Even if there are fewer layers within the organization, staff members may disagree about what is appropriate and what is not. This may lead to informal, backroom bickering that is not productive. Again, the librarian who is interested in using the blog in a new way may ultimately decide that it is not worth the effort.

As we can see, overly controlled environments can dampen innovation, so pulling back controls may be useful. But a lack of control also presents risks to the larger organization. Anyone who has spent any time online knows that there is a dark side to social media, and the web in general. Rude comments on blog posts are not unusual. Edited photos of celebrities, politicians and others are so regular that when one sees a strange photo, the first question asked is whether it has been Photoshopped. Viewers no longer trust what the eyes see. The global, open forum provided by the web and the ease of use and immediacy provided by social media present risks for organizations and individuals. Many times these risks do not focus on overtly rude and inappropriate comments or images. Often, they revolve around private or personal comments that enter the workplace.

For example, in 2010, a sociology faculty member named Gloria Gadsden was removed from campus at East Stroudsburg University of Pennsylvania after joking on Facebook about killing students (Miller, 2010). It is unlikely that university administrators thought that Ms Gadsden would actually take action against students, but following violence on other campuses, administrators probably felt compelled to act once students brought this to their attention. The college administration could not appear to ignore a potential threat.

Similarly, Kimberley Swann a 16-year-old receptionist at Ivell Marketing and Logistics Limited in Clacton, UK was fired for posting on Facebook that her job was boring (Sky News, 2009). This may feel like overreaction by managers, but it highlights the disconnect between what employees and management may consider appropriate.

A more high-profile suspension was that of US news anchor and syndicated columnist Roland Martin who was suspended by news network CNN following a tweet he made during the US Super Bowl. He wrote, "If a dude at your Super Bowl party is hyped about David Beckham's H&M underwear ad, smack the ish out of him! #superbowl." Complaints calling this tweet insensitive and promoting violence started rolling in to CNN almost immediately. CNN could not afford to look as if they supported Martin's statements, so they took action. Martin offered an apology (Carr, 2012).

Organizations also face concerns over the release of information that may damage operations. In the days before social media, the distribution of internal or proprietary information was not so easy. Today, a click can send it worldwide. A prime example occurred in 2010 when the Israeli Defense Forces had to call off an operation because a soldier revealed the mission's location, day and time (Waghorn, 2010).

Managers may also face difficulties in controlling messages about their organization. The Obama administration learned this in the spring of 2011 following a raid by US special forces troops on a compound in Pakistan that housed terrorist leader Osama Bin Laden. This raid resulted in Bin Laden's death and the end of a nearly decade-long manhunt. Following Bin Laden's death, President Barack Obama prepared to address the world, but the news had already been leaked. It was leaked by a government bureaucrat name Keith Urbahn who tweeted, "So I'm told by a reputable person they have killed Osama Bin Laden. Hot damn" (Pasetsky, 2011). By the time President Obama gave his speech, the media were already in a frenzy over the news.

Media agencies have also needed to address the role of social media in reporting. For instance, the BBC has instructed its reporters and producers that news should be broken through the newsroom and not through Twitter. The BBC recognized that tweets during an ongoing event, such as a trial, may be very valuable as part of their coverage, but when a major event happens, like the verdict of the trial, that event should be sent through the BBC's standard coverage first and not through Twitter (Plunkett, 2012).

These examples highlight just some of the challenges faced by organizations. Bogdan Dumitru (2009) created a list of social media risks to corporations, which is adapted here for libraries:

- *Organizational reputation*: Staff represent the library in global communication, so the ways that they interact reflect back on the library for good or ill. Misstatements on controversial issues, insensitivity to people and populations, indelicate interjections into religious discussions, and oversteps in political debates can pull a library into unneeded distraction and controversy.

- *Involuntary information leakage*: Library staff can also make accidental missteps by letting out information that for legal or strategic reasons should be kept out of the public eye. Posts or comments around HR decisions or the hiring process should be kept out of social media. Libraries that are governed by boards of trustees or other municipal structures need to take care what and how they post about decisions that need to be made within the governing structure.

- *Intellectual property risks*: A great deal of the content on social media sites revolves around use of other people's intellectual property. This may involve posting quotes, book covers, images and music. Fair use guidelines can be blurry. Libraries need to support authors, artists and creators of information, and we can do this by helping to highlight their work. However, we also need to be careful we are following these guidelines. This includes ensuring that appropriate procedures are in place to handle images and recordings from events held in the library.

- *Data theft*: While libraries do not handle as much highly sensitive information as a bank, libraries do need to be aware of the realities of identity theft and be careful with patron information. Most library integrated systems have names, addresses, reading habits and other personal information about library users. This information may not be directly connected to social networking tools, but managers should be aware of who has access to this information and how easily it could be shared.

- *Spam, phishing, malware and network vulnerability*: Any time a library's network accesses the rest of the internet there is a degree of risk from malicious software and individuals. Social media can be a delivery mechanism for malware and also for apps that collect user data. Most of these risks are manageable and generally minor, but managers should have an awareness of such risks.

- *Maintenance costs and productivity loss*: There is a cost in staff time related to social media. Most of the time it may be worth it, but it is a cost none the less. For social tools to be useful, they must have a regular flow of information, which takes time commitment. Additionally, staff may get pulled into their own personal social media accounts and spend "on-the-clock" time on their own accounts.

Librarians and staff members can easily and cheaply communicate globally, but a tweet or post does not need to go global to cause problems for organizations. Several of the above risks can be solved with updated anti-virus software, a decent firewall and IT staff that keep up with the demands of operating a local network. But several of the risks— namely organizational reputation, involuntary information leakage, intellectual property risks, maintenance costs and productivity loss—are softer risks that cannot be solved through technology. As discussed in Chapter 1, these are the people problems that require more graceful solutions and ongoing management.

When faced with these risks, managers and leaders face the temptation of being heavy handed and stamping out innovation. The simplest way to control problems is to set limits. Generally, limits take the form of rules that either prevent access so that only specific people can use technologies or reduce functionality so that technology can be used only in predefined ways. Another common solution is to establish punishments for misuse. This becomes a limit-by-fear approach. Instead of offering guidance, managers create an environment where it is easier to avoid the technology than risk punishment for misuse. The result of these limits is that technologies become less useful and less adaptable.

The conundrum of control faced by managers is that the use of social media tools requires some kind of form and context. But the more structures that are put in place around these tools, the more people and energy are required to manage them. There is a friction cost. The life of a social media tool cannot be planned. It cannot be managed. If it is to meet changing needs, it needs to grow and adapt along with the needs. However, social media tools can be coordinated and given context. Staff members need to be able to make sense around tools so that they feel comfortable innovating and rethinking how technology applies to the organization.

Managers and leaders must recognize that a healthy tension exists between focus and innovation. Reaching organizational goals requires planning, which requires some degree of focus. Budgets and actions must align in order to move forward. Focus is required to keep staff members from moving in a thousand different directions at the same time. Organizational members cannot reach a goal if they cannot see the goal. Nevertheless, innovation often requires us to blur this focus. Organizational members may need to move away from one goal in order to invent a new goal. The rebellious voice that is willing to point out a problem and offer a solution is the voice that makes change happen. The process of refocusing can be slow and painful. Managers must live within this tension or innovation will never really be realized.

Success for social media is tied to the willingness of organizational members to participate. Managers can require them to write blog posts, but any post that is compulsory will be safe, neutered and meaningless. The most powerful use of social media is by engaged staff members who see an opportunity to make a difference. Managers cannot force people to want to make a difference. The best option is to create an environment where people feel supported and want to make a difference.

Coordination tools and social media

Chapter 2 outlined the library as a loosely-coupled system and how the coordination tools of budgets, policies, participation rules and organizational culture allow individuals to come together and accomplish work. Coordination tools allow organizational members to make sense of their place within the larger whole. Knowledge about the organization is filtered through the prism of coordination tools. Did the organization reach its goals? What are the most significant obstacles to success? Is this a good place to work? What technology is useful? Who fixes problems? Who causes problems? Who is allowed to speak up about problems? These are all questions that coordination tools help answer.

Coordination tools can be utilized to create an environment where cooperation, collaboration and engaged use of the technology can thrive. Naturally, this is often easier said than done. Managers and leaders must work within the organization they find. Pushing a closed organization toward openness before it is ready is a recipe for disaster. It is akin to a body rejecting a transplanted organ. Organizational members who are accustomed to living in an environment where openness results in negative consequences will be scared to death of sudden openness. Movement toward change needs to fit the particular library's culture and follow a trajectory that makes sense. Managers and leaders must recognize where their organization stands and move forward appropriately. Examining the organization's coordination tools can be a way to initiate change.

Policies and engagement

Policies are often the coordination tool that comes to mind first when we consider the operation of organizations. When questions arise, organization members ask, "what does the policy say?" In many situations, individuals desire clarity, and that is exactly what policies appear to give. As new initiatives are put in place, managers and leaders often write policies, which can feel like accomplishment. The written word, capturing ideas, presenting the rules to make change a reality. Of course, anyone who has worked in an organization knows the truth, which is that policies are rarely consulted. They are often forgotten almost as quickly as they are written. Practices change over time, new technologies arise, and policies become separated from reality.

The problem is that leaders and managers often expect policies to do the work of people. They expect policies to remind people of the proper approach to technology and to help clarify ambiguous situations, when these responsibilities should really fall to managers. Policies, as written documents, are never good at reminding anybody of anything, and they rarely offer guidance through ambiguity.

This is not to say that policies are unimportant. The most important purpose for any policy is during the implementation stage of a new service or technology. This is when policies have the most potential to drive change. The creation of the policy itself is a vital step in fostering change. Policies should not just arise from the minds of leaders like Athena from the head of Zeus. The process in writing the policy can initiate change. A policy written in secret and dumped on organizational members will be ignored or will cause a revolution. It does not foster healthy change.

The process around creating policies will depend greatly on the size of the organization. Organizational leaders will be in the best position to define the needed process. No matter the process, a first step to creating a useful social media policy is to get the right people at the table. Assign this task to the people who are most involved and most knowledgeable. The makeup of this group will vary widely from organization to organization. This group must spend time gathering input from people not at the table. The writers also need to understand the needs of staff and library users. In addition to understanding needs, the process of reaching out to staff members starts to build awareness that change is coming. After the writers have started to gather input, they should review existing policies to discover gaps and to consider whether existing policies should be rewritten. Writing by committee can be painful. Sometimes multiple authors must write together, and other times, a single author can be assigned the task. But ideas must reach a computer screen somehow. After the writers have created a draft policy, this should be shared within the organization in order to get feedback and catch any potential problems. After this input has been incorporated, the policy can be sent up for approval from the director or governing board as appropriate.

Larger organizations have the potential to be constantly editing and rewriting policy documents. Creating a highly involved process covering many organizational members may not be possible, because too much time and energy will be spent writing policies. In contrast, smaller organizations may not have the people to devote to a highly involved writing process. This may fall to one or two people. Managers will need to weigh the impact of a policy and level of energy involved with writing the policy. As social media have low barriers to entry and therefore could be utilized by all members of the organization, a more involved and high-profile process may be warranted. The more attention given to the process, the greater the impact the policy will have.

Once the policy has been finalized, the policy should become a tool for fostering conversation and change. The policy should be sent around and promoted to turn attention to the change it represents. Managers should highlight new features emphasized by the policy and use this discussion as a way to move change forward. The initial creation and implementation of the policy offers the widest splash and most significant instance for shifting an organization.

Once in place, policies are most powerful when in the hands of a manager or leader. When members of a department are experimenting with a new tool, managers can hand them the policy, point out ways to avoid pitfalls, and emphasize the benefits that social media can bring to the organization. The ongoing relevance of any policy is really in the hands of managers and leaders. It is up to them to keep the approach and values defined in a policy at the forefront of the day-to-day activities of the organization.

Most libraries already have some sort of technology-related policy. A wave of policies were put in place in the late 1990s and early 2000s focusing on email, internet use and chat rooms, all of which were cutting-edge at the time. As social media tools have grown and evolved, many organizations have not devoted energy to updating existing policies. Keeping policies updated takes energy and time that most libraries do not have, especially considering that policies are often put away and forgotten. One may ask, "why update policies?" Updating policies can be useful for several reasons.

First, a significant policy revision is the first step to increasing the use of new technologies. In fact, the most important purpose for policy documents is to promote use. Even though social media may be relatively inexpensive, most libraries have already invested in computers, network access and the time of their staff. Managers and leaders should want these resources used to advance our missions as much as possible, and social media can definitely add value. Too often, staff members view policies as lists of rules defining inappropriate actions. Policies should actually be the opposite. Policies should enable action by defining how tools can be useful and how they will help to accomplish organizational goals.

Second, a policy revision can help organizational members clarify organizational values. Policies are essentially codified value statements. Policies connect values to actions. When managers use policies to threaten staff members with consequences for breaking a list of rules, they communicate values. They indicate that the organization will not support innovation. When policies define an environment for success, they communicate a desire for continuous improvement.

Third, a policy revision can educate staff members about legal concerns. Even though most policies overly focus on legal issues, legalities still remain important. Different laws will come into play depending on the type of library. A librarian or staff member at a university library with a focus on the curriculum may relate to users differently than a public library that may technically be part of local government. The concerns of a children's librarian may differ from those of an adult services librarian. The country, region, type of library and user community will greatly influence the legalities around social media. No matter the legal requirements, policy writers should take great care in crafting the legal wording. This is the type of language that can easily scare staff members and discourage use. Whenever possible, writers should try to offer examples and guidance to help staff members avoid falling into legal problems.

Finally, a policy revision can define or redefine responsibilities. Are social media organized at the department level or is there a single social media presence for the entire library? Are social media the responsibilities of individual staff members? Who can approve new social media tools? Most organizations have already answered these questions through exploration of the tools, but the answers may not be reflected in policy. Writers must be careful not to go too far with defining workflows in policy documents. Policies can be difficult to change, and workflows often need to be flexible.

Staff members will initially think about social media policy in relation to policies they already know or to policies that they *think* they know. The most prominent in most organizations are policies relating to email, which is a tool used many times each day. The degree of regulation, acceptable personal use, and degree of support around email will affect the ways that individuals see social media. As social media tools evolve, newer tools (such as Pinterest or Tumblr) will be viewed from the framework of older tools (like blogs or Facebook). The ways that managers and organizational members rely on these tools to accomplish goals will set the tone for the adoption of new tools. A policy revision can help to solidify these approaches if they are healthy or can help to change them if they are not desirable. In any case, staff members will connect existing policies and existing technologies to new technologies.

Crafting a Social Media Policy

Many templates for social media policies exist. It can be useful to review policies of peer libraries if possible. Almost all social media policies will include a purpose statement or statement of goals. This statement should be purposefully broad and must promote use of the technology. The first sentences of the policy are the sentences most likely to be read by staff members. For example:

> Social media sites such as blogs, wikis, Facebook and Twitter are important tools in advancing our library's mission by allowing librarians and staff members to easily offer services to library users. Our library views the active use of social media as being vital to our success in the future through improving the educational needs of library users and improving communication between librarians and staff members within the library.

A purpose statement may want to connect social media back to other established practices:

> The ethic of customer service and friendliness that is at the heart of our face-to-face interactions should guide our application of social media.

To clearly outline the benefits that social media can provide, a benefits statement can be included as part of the purpose or can be included as a separate section of the policy:

> Social media provide the following benefits to our library:
>
> - two-way communication between librarians and library users;
> - easy communication of library services and programming to the community;
> - online learning space where individuals can share information;
> - opportunities to support the library's existing online research databases.

The list of benefits will vary depending on the library and the approach to social media. The benefits statement is an opportunity to highlight the potential for social media and give innovation a push forward. A policy may need to define "social media" just to be clear about the types of sites to which the policy applies:

> *Social media* refers to websites or smart phone apps that allow for the immediate publication of information on the internet and for immediate user comment. Often social media sites allow users to share postings, links, images or other information between staff members and the general public. This may include social networking sites such as Facebook or LinkedIn, blog sites such as Blogger or Wordpress, micro-blogging sites such as Twitter, or video sharing sites such as YouTube.

The level of necessary definition will depend on the organization. If the goal is to encourage use from less savvy users, including detailed definitions may be appropriate.

Following definitions, a policy statement may need to outline use guidelines. If done incorrectly, these will read like a list of edicts not to be violated. If done correctly, these can create a framework around the use of social media. For example:

> Social media enable our library to improve our community through seamlessly sharing information and promoting our services to library users. The following approaches to social media should guide our use of social media:
>
> - The ethic of high-quality customer service that is central to our face-to-face service should guide our online services.
> - User privacy is at the heart of our mission. In supporting this mission, we will take great care in sharing information about users and users' reading habits.

- As a learning-centered institution, we believe in and support the copyright of authors, musicians, filmmakers and others who create information.

- Any librarian or staff member who recognizes a need that social media can address should work within his or her department to implement the social media tool.

- Librarians and staff members should not fear difficult topics as long as they are posted for the appropriate audience and introduced in the proper context. For instance, some topics may be appropriate on a page for an adult book group that may not be appropriate for a page designed for teens or children.

- Our library encourages librarians and staff members to be consumers of social media to enrich their lives. When using social media for personal or professional activities that are not directly tied to their position in the library, librarians or staff members should indicate that they do not represent the library in postings referring to the library.

- Our library seeks to create an open and safe environment for information sharing. User comments on library social media sites that are deemed to be combative, offensive or threatening will be removed by the library staff member responsible for managing the library's social media presence.

The list of guidelines can easily become quite lengthy, so writers should take care to include only those guidelines that are deemed absolutely necessary. Lists that are too long and cluttered detract from actually having staff members understand the larger goals of the policy, actually reading the policy, and making a change in actions.

The writers may also include a less formal set of practices than the official guidelines, such as best practices for social media. Best practices tend to be situational and therefore included and excluded as circumstance dictates. A best practices statement may state:

> The following list of best practices may be useful to social media users within our library.
>
> - Departments within our library may wish to write their own use guidelines for social media tools. This may help librarians and staff members understand how social media can advance the department's goals.
> - Communication between our staff members is one way we stay effective and provide quality services. Authors and administrators of the library's social media sites should communicate with supervisors and other department members about any issues of concern or needs that might arise.
> - Librarians and staff members should try to avoid posting to social media when angry. Negative patron interactions or hotly debated issues can charge us up and lead to a strongly written blog post, tweet or Facebook post that we might not have written in a calmer state of mind.
> - Librarians and staff members who are posting their personal opinions on their personal social networking sites can use the following easy approaches to differentiate their views from their view as a library staff members. They can simply say,
>   - "I work for at the library, but this is my own personal opinion."
>   - "I do not speak for my library, but my own personal opinion is…"

- Librarians and staff members may share information on controversial topics. When doing this, they may also need to identify their role as within the library. This may be done in "about" statements on individual social media pages. They can do this by saying something like,
  - "As a reference librarian, it is important to share sources on…"
- Library staff members should ensure that at least one other staff member has access to social media sites used by our library in case the site's primary author/administrator is not available.

The library's social media policy should be differentiated from the procedures used to post information to social media sites. Writers sometimes feel tempted to include procedural information in policy statements. Some recommendations state that a library should have one policy for the public and one for staff. This flies in the face of transparency and sets up confusing situations where staff may misinterpret the public or internal policies. If writers would like to help clarify actions, then they may wish to create a procedure document to clarify actions.

A procedure defines and organizes a process. This can be very important when coordinating and standardizing actions between many people. The long-term impact of written procedures is to prevent change. They capture and cement actions. This can be useful when an activity is complex and has too many steps for an individual to remember or when multiple individuals must work together on the activity. Written procedures can also be useful when activities may have a large degree of variation, and there is a need to unify action to ensure quality. High-impact activities like computer system implementations or management of personal user data may require precise procedures to ensure that information is managed correctly. Procedures will naturally evolve and change over time, so written documents will go out of date and need to be updated.

Procedures around social media can be helpful depending on the actual service provided. In my library, we have written procedures for posting our podcasts, because there are many steps involved including editing the MP3 file, uploading the MP3 file, updating the XML file, posting the XML file to the server, updating the appropriate page on the library's website, and writing a blog post about the podcast. On top of these steps, there are three different people who post podcasts, so there is a need to ensure all three follow the same steps. Procedures may be useful to identify appropriate subjects to write about on a blog, handling inappropriate comments by users, and even in creating new social media sites that represent the library.

Impact of budgets

Policies and budgets are the most formal of the coordination tools. Budgets are especially formal in publicly supported libraries. Budgets are often public documents that are developed and published at the end of one year, then implemented following strict accounting standards. They are intended to make expenditures transparent to members of the organization and the public.

Interestingly, many social media implementations exist outside of the budget process. Starting a Facebook page, Twitter account or a blog requires no additional costs. Many libraries have technology committees that oversee budget expenditures on software and hardware. Social media implementations often bypass this process because they have no additional costs. They are "free." Of course, "free" requires staff time, hardware and network infrastructure. Just because there is not a line in the library budget identified as "Facebook" does not mean that there is not a cost to the many Facebook pages created by the library.

Social media avoid centralized management by being outside of the budget process. Sites may pop up all over the place because organizational members can start them with just a computer and internet connection. The lack of centralization may present issues for managers. Generally, erring on the side of innovation and experimentation may be the best practice, but there may be a point where every department, every project or every staff member is creating individual pages. This can get out of hand. This may be especially true in larger libraries with more staff members and a greater number of projects. The more pages that are created, the more likely these pages will go dormant and obscure current goals. Identifying and managing the different social media tools to eliminate unnecessary pages can be a challenge to managers.

One budgetary action that managers can take to support social media is to carve out time for staff to use them. This may come from hiring individuals to implement social media or from releasing staff members from existing work in order to prioritize social media. Providing hardware such as desktop computers, mobile devices or handheld tablets are additional budgetary approaches to improving access to social media.

Organizational culture and participation rules: creating a shared vision

Legal scholar and internet guru Lawrence Lessig (1999) uses the legal term "latent ambiguity" in reference to an unclear legal situation where existing law no longer speaks directly to new circumstances changed by technology or time. For instance, the meanings of freedom of speech or freedom of the press, which are protected in many countries, have had to be reconsidered with the rise of the internet. Past applications of law may present ambiguities for present situations where any citizen can communicate instantly and globally.

Social media tools evolve so quickly that they guarantee ambiguities. In December 2011, Facebook adopted its timeline feature, radically changing its "wall" interface. Before the timeline, a user's wall contained a summary of recent activity, but activities from previous years were difficult to find. Facebook users knew that past comments, funny photos and political statements were technically available in Facebook, but they were difficult to access. The timeline changed all of this. Instantly, every interaction with Facebook was organized by date. The default setting was to make all content available to each user's friends. Although users had the option to hide past activities, they had to do this post by post, which was cumbersome. Some individuals who started using Facebook in college back when parents and employers were not able to access the site were mortified to know that previously hidden information was now easily available. Some of these individuals may have worked in libraries and had some inflammatory remarks buried away in their online past when the Facebook timeline was not foreseen.

The hottest social networking site of 2012 was Pinterest (Figure 5.1). This site allows users to share images and sites using a virtual pin-board. It is open, visual and addictive. At the beginning of 2011, the site was not on the radar. By 2012, it was heavily used and enabling sharing on a massive scale. A library's social media policy could not possibly have addressed Pinterest in 2011. Unless a librarian was about to invent this site (and it was not invented by a librarian), then there would have been no way to write a policy around it.

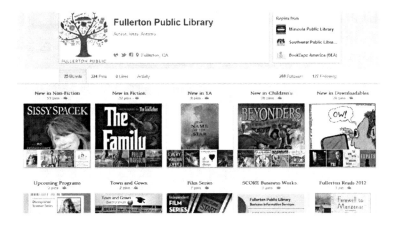

Figure 5.1 Fullerton Public Library's use of Pinterest to highlight new additions to its collection

The Facebook timeline and Pinterest are two examples of changes that had significant impact in the social media world that could not be easily predicted. Countless social media sites exist across the web, and countless more will be invented within a relatively short time. The formal processes behind policies and budgeting cannot respond quickly enough to address these tools directly. The only real option for organizations is to enable organizational members to adapt to new situations and use their own judgment. This is the role of organizational culture around social media. As discussed in Chapter 2, organizational culture fills in the gaps where formal policies and procedures fall short. This is the realm of values, habits, symbols, history and norms. This is also a realm that can be difficult to change.

A policy document that emphasizes use and is promoted widely is a first step toward creating a healthy social media culture. Promoting successes through awards or mentions in the organizational newsletter is another step. When managers highlight a successful social media tool, they are not just giving a pat on the back those who are responsible. They are communicating values to the rest of the organization. They are saying, "this is ok." Devoting time for training sessions or funding to send staff to workshops are other visible ways to support social media and push the culture.

Punishment is the most serious way to poison a culture, especially punishment around innovation. The staff member who is punished for creating a social media site without permission will always be remembered. Of course, punishments do not just come from managers. They can also come from coworkers. In 2004, when our library implemented its first blogs, I had to beg and beg to get other librarians to use them. One of our senior librarians put up a post that was written entirely in uppercase letters. Several librarians complained about this in the middle of a department meeting. They said that it was poor etiquette and that she should change the post. I was ecstatic that she actually posted, so I tried to deflect their comments. But, the damage was done. I was not able to get that librarian to post to our blogs for several more years.

The participation rules around social media send a message about the role of this technology to the organization. As discussed in Chapter 2, participation rules exist between policy and organizational culture. These are the written and unwritten rules about who gets to do what. Lessig (1999) discusses participation rules in terms of the architecture of the technology. The code that creates the technology hardwires the values of the organization. The code determines who gets access and what they can do online. Architecture is the formalization of participation rules.

For instance, the job classifications of staff members who have access to social media sites communicate the values of the library. If only reference librarians have access to the library's Facebook page, then this communicates the page's purpose. If the page is used only to promote cultural events, this would be a different purpose. The individuals who are designated as page administrators on Facebook would also communicate status. This is not to say that all employees must have equal access to all social media sites. However, managers and leaders must be aware that if a particular page is given a particular purpose, they should be listening to staff at all levels for other needs and find ways to address those needs.

Participation rules often define the level of service that a library will provide. Does the library provide a standardized, fast food approach where one size fits all or does it provide an individualized approach where services adapt to the needs of the specific user? Employees who are allowed to act within their judgments are more able to address the specific needs of the user. Employees who feel limited will only offer a standardized service. Clearly, managers must strike a balance as most libraries do not have staffing levels that allow for individualized service for every patron.

Managers can push organizational culture by examining participation rules and by trusting organizational members with the power to act. Managers need to protect innovation from the slings and arrows of those who may feel threatened. Social media focus on sharing and engaging users around ideas. The ideas that matter most to communities are often ideas that are the most controversial or the most difficult. Organizational culture should give staff a sense of what is appropriate and what is not. It should also empower them to take risks and not to fear difficult situations. Many staff members will avoid conflict and avoid risk and this will give the library a neutered voice on the web.

Management and coordination

Most social media tools grow up organically within libraries. Individuals take ownership and implement them. The tool then becomes defined as the domain of that person. If Eric is the library's blogger, then the blog will be viewed as serving Eric's goals rather than the goals of the library. Even worse, other staff members may feel that they are stepping on Eric's toes or crossing into his turf if they try to post to the blog. A manager can encourage participation by defining the ways that people will work together to move a task forward.

Sometimes staff members may be willing to participate and they may recognize content that could be shared. They may even feel comfortable with the technology, but they are unsure how to get access. Defining some sort of management structure around social media helps ease some of these concerns. As an organization, the library needs to make decisions about how social media will be utilized, which often focuses on defining the individuals who will have responsibility for the tools.

Figure 5.2 defines a general structure around social media that includes a human filter. This example uses blogs, but the structure could work for almost any social media tool. In this example, a staff member consults with the director of public relations prior to posting to the blog. If the item is newsworthy or if it is something that should follow traditional media channels, then the PR staff can take it and promote it on the library's news blog and via press release.

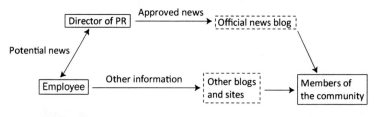

Figure 5.2   **News channel structure**

If the item is not as newsworthy, then the staff member can post it directly to the library's social media sites. For instance, a new reading program may be something that deserves more attention from the organization and therefore will receive a formal media announcement. In contrast, a story about new resources for job seekers may be a nice blog post, but not warrant a full media release.

This structure is fairly useful for organizational members who are new to social media and may not have the confidence to jump in and post. As they use the technology, the structures can become more informal as most staff members will come to recognize whether an informational item is newsworthy and will consult the PR office only if they are unsure. Nevertheless, this sort of approach is especially useful for new social media users because it defines whom to approach with questions about content.

Figure 5.3 outlines an open structure for managing social media. This example uses blogs, but any social media tool could be substituted. This structure is a free-for-all where any employee can access any social media tool. This open approach could be useful for small libraries, where employees spend time together and can discuss how to use social media on a case-by-case basis. This open structure can become the default when social media sites have grown up out of experimentation.

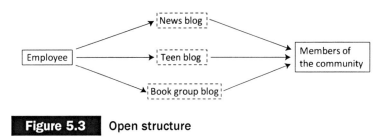

Figure 5.3   Open structure

In larger libraries, social media sites are often initiated at the department level, which makes sense considering that goals and audience may vary between departments. Figure 5.4. defines a departmental structure for managing social media. Sometimes employees may move between departments, so employees may be granted access to multiple sites in multiple departments depending on their job responsibilities. The example in Figure 5.3 can be used for any social media tool. This figure indicates that the department head is the person responsible for managing social media tools, but this responsibility could be handled differently in different departments. The formal manager need not be the manager of social media on top of other duties. However, this structure does depend on a single person keeping track of tools and individuals with access.

With the proliferation of social media options, managing multiple sites within a single department can be difficult. Just managing the basics, which might include a blog, Facebook, Twitter and Google+, can be a handful. Throw in Flickr and YouTube, and it can be a nightmare. Figure 5.5 defines an

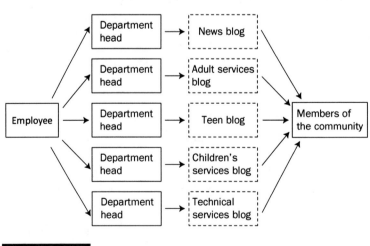

Figure 5.4   Departmental structure

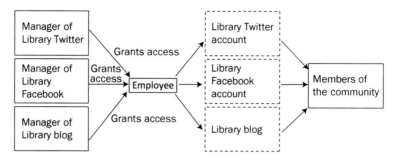

Figure 5.5 Structure to manage multiple sites

initial structure for managing multiple sites within a department. In this example, each tool is given a manager who would be responsible for keeping track of content and employee access. Libraries may end up identifying individuals who are the local experts on certain tools, and the staff must recognize how to route information to that person for inclusion. This means that a degree of awareness is required by the larger group members. Some software packages help departments manage multiple sites. For instance, the Hootsuite application allows staff to publish to multiple Facebook, Twitter, LinkedIn and Foursquare accounts.

In larger organizations, an additional management structure may be necessary to facilitate communication between departments. This may simply require a social media management committee where social media managers can meet with PR staff to discuss messages and outreach efforts. As described in Chapter 4, libraries can learn from journalism in terms of exploring issues that are important to their communities. Another idea that can be stolen from journalism is that of the front page or editorial meeting. These vary between media outlets, but their essential purpose is to list out the main news items of the day and prioritize them to ensure proper coverage. Managers and leaders in libraries may not want to borrow this literally, but it would not be overly difficult to include discussions of issues covered by social media at department or staff meetings. Coordinating topics ensures that social media sites do not focus overly on one topic while neglecting others. This can also allow staff members to talk about how they will approach specific topics and solicit ideas about other resources that may be tied to issues.

Motivating employees to use

There is a tendency for managers and leaders to think broadly across the organization. They imagine all employees accessing social media tools and using them directly as part of their jobs. The reality is that familiarity with tools and usage of social media tools will be unevenly distributed across the organization. This mirrors usage of social media in general. Power users may make up only 20 percent of users within a social network, but they generate a vast majority of the content (Hampton et al., 2012). Some staff members will generate a great deal of content and others will generate much less. This is fine, and it may be something that managers cannot easily change. Successful social media utilization means engagement in meaningful issues, which cannot be forced upon library staff. In addition, managers should not be overly concerned if one or two individuals dominate a particular social media tool. This is just a reflection of staff personalities.

When it comes to workflows and processes, managers can live with the uneven distribution of work, but, as has been discussed in earlier chapters, having more voices involved with social media is an advantage to the organization. Thus, managers should work to grow participation. Writing policy, shifting culture, addressing participation rules, and outlining structures can increase participation. Training is the final piece to foster change. Training most often focuses on the technical aspects of using social media sites. Creating accounts, logging in, and navigating around new tools clearly take a priority, as new sites cannot be used if staff members do not know the nuts and bolts of using the site. However, training should not neglect the discussions around goals and content. Staff should develop an understanding around how the new social media tool accomplishes organizational goals. This understanding pushes the larger organizational culture and builds connections for staff members between purpose and tools. This is important because this understanding provides the foundation for decision making. It keeps staff focused on accomplishing goals, but it also enables them to recognize opportunities for innovation and growth in the future.

One understanding staff members should have is whether they access tools as individuals or share group logins. Does the library have a corporate voice? This may depend on the particular social media site. Some sites have rules against sharing logins. Most have ways to create pages for the entire organization. On some sites, it will make sense to have a single voice, while others will not. For instance, it may not make sense for every staff member to have a Flickr account for photos as part of their employment. It would make more sense to have a library-wide Flickr account so that all publicly shared photos are together under one account. On the other hand, blog posts tend to make more sense when attributed to a single author, and most blogging software makes it possible to assign individual accounts for each staff member.

Training is time-consuming and expensive. Most libraries are not able to close services in order to train all staff members. This is why training is often focused on key users with the hope that knowledge about the innovation will travel through the organization. In his foundational work on innovation, *Diffusion of Innovations*, Everett Rogers (1995) describes the three types of knowledge about innovations within an organization. First, he describes "awareness-knowledge," where individuals know that the innovation exists and start to see the benefits that the innovation may bring. For instance, one department may notice another department's blog and how easily the blog allows for the publication of information.

Second, Rogers outlines "how-to knowledge," which is knowledge about the technical and mechanical process needed to make the innovation work. This is important because staff members must evaluate whether the threshold for use is too great to make the innovation worth pursuing. For instance, staff may recognize that a podcast may be a useful innovation for their department. But, after investigating, they may decide that editing MP3 files, managing server space, updating XML files, or dealing with podcast software may not be worth their time and resources.

Finally, Rogers defines "principles knowledge," which are the foundational concepts tied to system functions. This theoretical knowledge allows staff members to connect an innovation with organizational goals. Principles knowledge is important, because this brings about the insight needed to recognize how a technological innovation can move organizational goals forward. Principles knowledge enables a broader understanding of the technology that can extend to new tools which may enable further innovation.

Often, innovations spread within the organization through the work of a single person. Rogers refers to this individual as an "innovation champion" who has successfully implemented an innovation and helps spread the innovation to other individuals and departments. Innovation champions are not typically managers. They are often risk-takers on the frontlines. When managers and leaders can recognize an innovation champion, they can empower the champion. Often, the innovation champion is the best person to lead training sessions and meet with departments during formal meetings where innovations may be discussed. Champions spread the word and act as symbols for innovation among the staff.

A simple way to encourage staff members to use social media is to create a schedule. This may feel heavy handed or artificial at first, but scheduling one person to be responsible for a site at different times of the day, week or month ensures use. A manager who is trying to establish a Facebook page, Twitter account or a new blog needs to ensure that content will move from staff in the library to the online world. Pages that are not updated regularly look abandoned and forgotten. Scheduling staff member time is a practical way to ensure that content is fresh. This is also a way to build knowledge within a group of staff members. Without a schedule, innovation champions and power users will contribute content but social media novices will be less likely to participate. When novices are assigned a time to post information to a social media tool, they will have to clear up technical questions and find content with value for the community. A lone staff member who wants to grow a new social media presence may find software like Hootsuite to be advantageous. Hootsuite allows for scheduled content, so that a month's worth of tweets or Facebook posts can be prepared ahead of time. This is a very useful way to ensure content is posted to pages.

Living with mistakes

As managers know, mistakes happen. While mistakes with social media can be quite public, they are unavoidable. Managers must be prepared to let mistakes go and carefully correct the mistakes that cannot be ignored. The goal of policy and infrastructure is to minimize mistakes. Spending time with novice users is important in order to give them guidance and encouragement. Managers and leaders should also attempt to keep an eye on social media tools so that they might catch mistakes before they can be noticed by the community.

If complaints are made by community members, managers must resist overreacting. Grievous violations of policy, serious inaccuracies or hateful comments should be addressed immediately. They should be removed and necessary apologies and needed disciplinary processes should be made. Extremely offensive violations are very rare, as most staff members recognize the line between insulting and appropriate language. Most problems will be minor and exist in gray areas. They should be handled carefully with proper perspective. Minor factual errors should be corrected by the authors that made them. Language that may be terse or overly harsh can be used as a learning opportunity for the future. Complaints from the public that are not about a grievous violation should be dealt with where the complaints originated. For example, a tweet from a user complaining about the length of library hours should be replied to with a tweet. If a user complains on Twitter, a manager should not look up the patron's name and call his or her house.

Additionally, complaints should be given the degree of attention that they deserve. The best way to turn a small complaint into a major issue is to overreact. Anyone who has spent any time reading blogs know that there will be comments that disagree with any post. Blog authors should resist replying to each comment. Authors should reply to thoughtful comments that further the conversation, but reason must be used. Of course, the best way to turn a major issue into a really major issue is to ignore it. Just because a complaint is made on social media, does not mean that it should not be taken seriously. Some tweets should find their way to the library director and department heads.

Social media can be a great communication tool, and staff training should include a discussion about effective communication. However, managers and leaders also must recognize that the best way to learn is from experience, which will mean some mistakes will be made. Most mistakes will be minor and should be utilized as opportunities for growth.

Finding collaboration, coordination and focus

Chapter 4 discussed many of the possible ways that social media can connect to organizational goals. This chapter has described the ways to build a framework that coordinates staff around these goals. The coordination tools that turn a group of individuals into a functional organization are instrumental in building social media into the fabric of employees' daily life. Policies, budgets, organizational culture and participation tools are the means used by managers and leaders to drive change. When social media are implemented but coordination tools do not reflect the technology's advantage, then the new technology will not be fully integrated into the core of the organization.

Most libraries recognize that one additional step to getting exposure to social media is the integration of these tools with the library's primary web presence. This integration is not just about visibility, but also about recognizing the impact that social media can have. Adding a social layer across a library site can be complicated depending on the size of library and the knowledge of the library's technology staff. Chapter 6 outlines some approaches to better integration.

6

Integrating with standard websites

Abstract: Managers and leaders must carefully consider how to connect their websites with social media tools. The integration of online sites can be difficult as resources are limited. Homepage design must consider content, navigation, layout and aesthetics. Such competing needs force designers to balance goals and priorities. It is also essential for designers to see things through the eyes of the user. Usability testing makes this possible. Usability tests gauge the effectiveness of site design. A website may be described as usable when a new user can navigate and understand it without special guidance or training. Usability studies can also be undertaken to test the integration of social media with standard websites. Site designers should consider which social media tools will be integrated across the entire website. The location of social media links will depend on the goals of the site. RSS feeds are a way to connect social media tools, create efficiencies for staff, and make content more sharable. Social media may also be integrated with online research tools such as integrated library systems and subscription databases. Inevitably, some social media sites will be abandoned. As such, managers should have in place strategies to preserve any connections made with users or to redirect users to the library's homepage.

Key words: social media, Facebook, Twitter, RSS, blogs, usability testing, homepage design

Introduction

There was a time when a library website was a nice addition to existing library services. An online presence was an exciting enhancement, but most services continued to function as they had for decades. In a short time, the library website evolved into an online brochure that had images, nice layouts and lots of text about the library. This iteration of website gave way to more service-driven, utilitarian sites that more seamlessly incorporated online catalogs, subscription databases and features such as chat or texting. Today, site managers are heavily incorporating social media. Library sites are evolving into mashups of locally-created content and externally-produced content held together by social-media-driven services.

Of course, simply adding social media tools to a library website does not make the site automatically better. Social media can be an inexpensive avenue to adding a range of functionality and services to a site, but adding functionality to a dysfunctional site may actually make a website less useful. Library staff, especially library website managers, must take a deep breath and carefully consider how best to incorporate social media into standard websites.

When does a social media tool warrant an appearance on the library homepage? As redesigning library homepages requires an investment of time and staff energy, site managers want to avoid integrating social tools into pages only to see social tools fall out of use and die away. Then the library site will contain dead links that detract from active and useful services. Thus, website managers may need to consider the threshold between experimental and established. When a social media tool is firmly established within the procedures and daily life of a library or department, then that social media tool should play a more prominent position on the library's website.

The homepage is the homepage

I started managing my library's website almost a decade and a half ago, when the web was relatively new and many libraries were happy just to have a presence online. This was a time when some sites were still coded by hand, and the first WYSIWYG editors were growing in dominance. Our college website was entering its first cooling-off stage after its birth. At this time, the website's molten lava, which had spewed forth a few years earlier, smoldered and consolidated into a more standardized and organized site.

When I walked through the door, I found that our library actually had a split web-personality. Within the library, all public and lab computers were set to a page generated by our integrated library system (ILS). The ILS had been online for many years, but the move to the web from dumb terminals was still relatively new. The page from the ILS was a simple one consisting of a table of links leading to the library's catalog and subscription databases. At the same time, the college's marketing department had set up a library landing page which was mostly text describing services and staff. This page was linked to the college's homepage. As a result, students found one homepage while in the library and another when outside of the library.

As one may imagine, library users found this very confusing. In classes, instructional libraries taught students how to navigate both pages. At the reference desk, librarians made sure students knew about both pages just in case they were researching from home. The page created by the marketing department was difficult to edit, because all changes needed to be sent through their staff. The page created by the library's ILS was locked behind screens and menus in the system which were difficult to access and update.

Creating a unified homepage for the library became my number one priority. After several discussions around the issues, our library established a partnership with our marketing department so that I could directly access the library page created through their designers. The administrative wranglings were less of a challenge than trying to prioritize the goals of our site. We outlined existing content, filled in missing content and identified user groups. Eventually, we worked to incorporate both library homepages together into a single site. The ILS-generated homepage became a secondary page just for research, while the marketing-generated homepage became the primary page for the library. At last, whether inside the library or at home, library users were able to access the same library site.

Over the years, our site has evolved a great deal as the technology has changed and our services have expanded. Nevertheless, the essential lesson of this initial library redesign is still relevant: the homepage is the homepage. The library's homepage is the entry point to the entire library site. The library's homepage establishes the site's navigation and organization. It must connect the library's various online instances into a coherent whole, providing an online identity and paths for users to take to access services.

As individuals and departments experiment with social media tools, managers and leaders must take care that competing homepages do not pop up. Individuals may establish their own sites and gateway pages that do not connect back to the library's primary web presence. In some cases, this may be needed for special populations or projects, but most of the time, social media and other sites should connect back to the general library site and make some effort to identify themselves as a piece of a larger site.

Land wars

In *Everything is Miscellaneous*, David Weinberger (2007) discusses visiting the prototype test store of the office goods giant Staples. The prototype store is where planners test the user experience in relation to signage, shelf organization and store floor-plan. Weinberger (2007: 5) outlines five limitations on physical space and store design:

- "In physical space, some things are nearer than others."
- "Physical objects can be only in one spot at any one time."
- "Physical space is shared."
- "Human physical abilities are limited."
- "The organization of the store needs to be orderly and neat."

Weinberger argues that the success of the shopper is determined by the relationship of the one thing that is needed to the many other things in the store. For most visitors to Staples, 99 percent of the items on the shelves hide the 1 percent that is useful. If a shopper enters the store in search of a printer cable, then all of the paper stock, office furniture, pens, highlighters and countless other supplies are just clutter getting in the way of the printer cables.

Weinberger's points were made about a physical store with physical items on its shelves, but they are absolutely applicable to the design of a library homepage. The design of any webpage is essentially a challenge of bounded space. Designers can adjust screen resolutions, font sizes and image sizes, but they must work within design limits, which are similar to those defined by Weinberger above. I adapt them as follows:

- *On a webpage, some items are closer to the top of the page*: The top of the page is nearer to our eyes, as it is the starting point. Higher priority items should be toward the top.

- *On a webpage, each segment of space can contain limited amounts of content*: The space on a homepage is limited, so there is only a finite amount of information that can be squeezed a on any single page.

- *Space on a page is shared*: Not only is the page limited, but there is a also a relationship between the different content on the page: the appearance of one piece of content affects how additional content is viewed. The more links we squeeze into one area, the smaller those links have to be. If a single image dominates a page or portion of a page, then it will necessarily hide other pieces of content on the page.

- *Human physical abilities are limited*: Most visitors do not have the time or patience to scrutinize carefully each and every link on a webpage. Their eyes move unevenly across the page, and there is no consistency in their knowledge of the terminology, jargon and purpose of the site. Nonetheless, library pages must strive to be usable and manageable.

- *Pages need to be neat and orderly*: A homepage must provide the visitor with an outline to the content of the rest of the site. If the site is to be successful, the homepage needs to offer order and direction.

Designing a library homepage is a battle over real estate. The top-left elements on a page are the most valuable, as Western eyes are trained to work from left to right and top to bottom. The further up the page a piece of content is located, the more likely it will be noticed and utilized by visitors. This is a balancing of competing needs. Designers must provide access to services, marketing of current or future services, administrative information, and information to support daily operations. Library managers and leaders should consider how the library homepage aligns with organizational goals. A visitor should be able to discern the library's priorities just by visiting its homepage.

When library managers consider social media and the library homepage, they need to keep a close eye on organizational priorities. The staff member who wants to transform the entire homepage into a blog or who says that the library's Facebook page could be the new library homepage may not have the right perspective on the library's larger goals. On the other hand, social media sites that do not connect to the primary library site are also a problem. Standard sites and social media pages must come together in a way that makes sense. Users who visit the library's standard site should be able to identify other ways to connect via social media. Library leaders should be cautious to prevent clusters of disconnected sites from popping up. This can confuse users, prevent users from discovering services, and waste staff time on maintaining multiple sites.

All library-wide social media tools should be present on the library's homepage. Department-level tools or tools dedicated to specific user groups should be prevalent on department pages, but probably not on the library's homepage. Of course, this decision is really up to the individual library. Some new services may need to be marketed on the library's homepage.

Thus, defining what should be and what should not be on a library's homepage is a land grab where limited space must be utilized wisely. There must be a process for making this decision. The site should not be the dominion of one manager who dictates the entire design of the homepage single-handedly. Input from users and staff should be at the heart of the process. The usability of the site is the ultimate goal.

Usability testing

A library homepage intermingles the following elements:

- *Content*: The actual text, images and ideas on the page.

- *Navigation*: The consistent system that allows users to move through the entire website.

- *Layout*: The spatial relationship between content.

- *Look and feel*: The color palette, graphics and affective impression of the site.

The essential test for any library homepage is whether or not a user can effectively utilize the site's services. This is a test of usability. Jakob Nielsen (2003) has demonstrated that usability is a testable quality for websites. Many libraries do not conduct usability testing and therefore do not test the impact of social media on usability. The best way to understand the impact of social media on an existing site is to perform a test and ask users to access new and existing services.

A usability study takes sample users and asks them to perform tasks that align with the site's goals. Testers record participant actions to identify wording, layout or design features that confuse users. If a site is truly usable, new visitors should be able to successfully navigate the site to accomplish tasks without instruction. Nielsen (2000) suggests that most usability studies need only a few users to discover the majority of usability obstacles. As few as five users are often enough, but many usability studies employ five to ten users to ensure that key obstacles are identified.

The following are the basic steps for conducting a usability study:

- *Test developers review and define site goals*: For most libraries, this would include locating resources, finding administrative information such as hours, and discovering upcoming programming.

- *Test developers create questions based on these goals*: Most goals only need to have one or two questions. Most usability studies are 10–15 questions.

- *Test developers decide how to capture data*: Some usability experts use screen-capture software such as Camtasia or Captivate so that they can go back and watch sessions in order to record each click a participant makes. If software is not available, then clicks can easily be recorded by hand. This may mean that a test moderator may be in the room to administer the test and a test recorder may be present to take notes and capture clicks. Many usability studies employ a talk-out-loud protocol, where users tell recorders where they are clicking. Participants can provide an explanation for their click to provide insight into how they are interpreting the site.

- *Test developers create scripts, release forms and procedures for the test*: This is especially important if there will be several people administering the test to participants. Scripts and procedures ensure that all information is provided to participants and that data are collected in similar ways.

- *Test developers test the test*: Before participants see questions, it is important that the questions actually test their goals. One way to do this is to run a test session with librarians. If the librarians cannot understand and successfully answer questions as designed, then there are problems with the questions. After the librarians, designers can run the test with other staff members who have less experience. If librarians and staff cannot successfully answer questions, this means that there are serious usability concerns with the site or that the questions are poorly written.

- *Test developers train test administrators and allow them to practice*: It is important that staff members giving the test understand how a session should flow and how the mechanics of the test come together.

- *Test developers recruit sample users*: Participants should be fairly representative of key user groups. However, usability is really a test of mechanics so many demographic variables will not greatly affect results. Demographics such as age group and language spoken may have greater impact than factors such as gender. Gifts or payments can be useful in attracting participants.

- *Moderators administer test to participants*: The test should be held in a conference room or classroom away from distractions. It is important to remind participants that this is not a test of their skills or knowledge. This is a test of the library's website.

- *Test developers compile and analyze data*: Data analysis can be time-consuming and tedious. Procedures for analysis should be developed to ensure that results are handled consistently over time to ensure that findings are credible.

This process is a qualitative approach that attempts to provide fuel for creativity. As such, test administrators, moderators and recorders should capture their feelings and ideas throughout the process. Inspiration is likely to strike in the midst of data collection as staff members follow the thinking of participants. As a qualitative approach, moderators should work to build a picture of the website through participants' eyes and be less concerned about data collection as a mechanical, objective process. Usability studies can be liberating for web designers who are seeking ways to make meaning as opposed to gathering data points.

Full-blown usability tests result in the most rigorous and systematic findings, but limited resources may not permit a full study. Staff limits or competing needs may keep a full study out of reach. If this is the case, informal tests may substitute. Any staff member can conduct an informal test simply by asking someone else to complete a task on the site and noting difficulties. This can be especially useful during information literacy classes or other library workshops. For example, one can ask students to take a few minutes and try to find an article posted on the library's Facebook page or an item from the collection. The leader can take note where individuals hit road blocks. This approach is efficient and cost-effective while still identifying weaknesses in usability. As time permits, this informal approach could be accomplished at the reference desk as well.

In terms of social media, usability studies can be especially helpful in exploring the connection between the standard website and social media sites. Moderators can ask participants to identify Facebook, Twitter, Google+, or other social media sites. They can be asked to find training videos on YouTube or find images on Flickr. They could be asked to find a podcast from a past event held in the library or a blog post about a community issue. If users are unable to perform these tasks successfully, then the points of failure represent needed change.

Usability tests can be useful in seeing how well users can navigate a social media tool on a library site, and usability tests can also help designers see how well users navigate within a social media site. If a department decides to use a new social media tool, knowledge about how well target audiences navigate within that tool may be useful. Library designers may not be able to redesign a site like Facebook or YouTube, but they can understand where their users get stuck and provide assistance in navigating the sites.

Usability studies give site designers insight into how users approach websites. A good study should generate data that lead to change. Ideally, such data will be gathered using a strong process, but usability data can be gathered through simple observation. The underlying point is that the ways that library websites are designed and the ways that library sites connect to social media should be designed using direct input and data from users.

Integrating across the sites

One of the large questions for library site designers is the degree of inclusion for social media. Will links to social media sites be included on every page of the site? Will they appear on the library's homepage only? Some staff members will say sites absolutely should be on every page, and others will see these links as cluttering up pages. Some library staff members would go so far as to prefer the library's homepage be transformed into a blog so that that discussions and valuable content are the first things that a user sees when visiting the site. Many libraries have done this, so it is not just a hypothetical example. Some libraries have put "read our blog" or "follow us on Facebook" in page banners that appear on every page. Deciding what to include and what to exclude can be difficult. It is unlikely that *every* social media tool can be included, or banners and homepages will be jam-packed with links.

The library's user population may provide some direction. If users are heavily active in social media, then links should have a priority, but most communities include a mix of active social media users and others who are less active. Usability testing can provide some direction as to how the inclusion or exclusion of links affects the larger goals of the site. However, usability focuses on the functionality of a site, and not what content *should* be included. Usability might tell you how well users can identify a link or whether the inclusion of a link prevents other links from being found, but it cannot dictate which site goals are a priority.

Managers may want to consider which social media tools reach the widest audience. If a library has a library-wide Facebook account, Twitter account or blog, then these should probably be present on the library's homepage and also as small links in the library's banner. Audience-specific pages such as Facebook pages for book groups should probably be included at lower levels of the library site on pages describing services to this audience. Site designers may want to find a way to highlight some of these audience-specific services on the homepage to increase their visibility, but this can be a balancing act depending on how many services exist.

As designers and managers consider how best to integrate social media across the site, they should remember that users come to sites for content and for services. They typically do not visit the site to find Facebook pages. When designers include links to social media tools, they should give visitors a reason to click. Instead of a link saying "Facebook," it might feel better to say "Connect with us on Facebook," "Keep up with us on Facebook" or "Follow the action on Facebook." The tone should reflect the library's relationship with users. Similarly, a link that says "read our blog" is about as bland and uninviting as possible. Blog links should reveal the purpose and content of the blog. Blogs are extremely flexible and content-rich. The ways that standard sites connect should reveal the blog's exciting content, even if the link includes only the blog title. A link might read "Visit our search tips blog," "Check out our sustainability blog," or "Read our new book blog." It is even better when blog posts can be incorporated into the site (see the following section on RSS feeds).

So far, this discussion on integrating social media into a site has considered linking users to social media accounts, which is probably the initial issue to consider. However, a more powerful way to connect standard sites and social media is to make library web content sharable. This is the step that helps libraries utilize the power of the social layer of the web. Imagine a local historical society that could use a single click to share a library's webpage about an upcoming lecture across Facebook, Twitter and other sites. This is perfectly possible and quite common. Most major news sites include "recommend this" links on news stories. Libraries could make every page of their sites sharable.

One of the most popular social widgets that makes page-level sharing possible is Addthis.com. This little gadget is free and fairly easy to use. It connects to over 300 social media networks and provides valuable analytic data about how content is shared. To sign up, a site administrator completes a form with information about the site and desired social networking tools. Addthis.com provides script code that can be pasted into the HTML of a webpage. Addthis.com has videos and other instructions on its site, with more detailed information on setting up the service and using its analytics. With one click, visitors will be able push content from the library site out to their networks.

Obviously, social media sites have an incentive to encourage readers to share content across their sites. When users push content, the sites benefit from the richness of discussions. Thus, many social media sites provide guidance in incorporating sharing buttons in standard sites. For instance, Facebook has a web developer site that offers instructions, code and useful approaches to incorporating Facebook buttons (see *http://developers.facebook.com/docs/guides/web/*). Like Facebook, Google+ has many developer tools (see, for example, the discussion on use of the +1 button to share content at *http://www.google.com/webmasters/+1/ button/*).

As discussed earlier in this book, many library social media sites are under-utilized ghost towns with few followers and little interaction. One reality around social media is that most people do not comment because they try to avoid public conflict. A critical mass of users must be reached before activity takes off. Some industry leaders have said that 1500 users is the base number required to reach heavy activity. This number may vary, but it is clear that site managers must have patience and perseverance to grow their audience. Integrating standard sites with social sites is a vital step to growing this audience.

Gaining efficiency through RSS

RSS may be the simplest and most powerful tool that most people don't know about. RSS allows for the easy sharing of content. RSS stands for "RDF site summary" or "really simple syndication" depending on who describes it, but for this discussion, the importance of RSS is in streamlining the sharing of content between platforms. RSS is a standardized form of XML, which basically means that it is a text file where information is labeled and described. Many social media tools can create RSS "feeds" to deliver a regularly updated flow of content. For instance, all blogs have an RSS feed, and when the blog gets updated, so does the RSS feed. Literally, the title, body, date and other information from the blog are added to the RSS feed. Blogs are not the only social media tools with RSS functionality. Podcasts, social bookmarking sites, wikis, social networking, microblogs and other sites all have RSS feed options.

The thing that makes RSS so useful is that the RSS file does not include design elements. Thus, content is separated from design, which is handy because that content can be imported into other sites. This is commonly known as a "mashup" between sites. The RSS feed can be used to pull articles, links, audio files and other content into webpages. Many news sites, like those of the *New York Times* or the BBC, have RSS feeds that allow users to pull content into other pages. Thousands of sites make RSS feeds available. Individuals can use readers such as iGoogle, Bloglines or Netvibes to view updated content from many sites all at once. Site designers can use RSS to incorporate social media into standard websites. Blog posts, tweets, podcasts and Facebook updates can be pulled into homepages. This is a great way to incorporate actual content into a site. Instead of having a link that says "read our blog," visitors can see actual titles from blog posts or names of podcast episodes.

RSS feeds are one reason that blogs remain so powerful. RSS allows the content of the blog to flow all around the web and be reviewed by many sets of eyes. The titles of blog posts provide useful previews for the content of the blog. Five to ten titles from a blog can easily be incorporated into a homepage as a bulleted list without sacrificing valuable space. When a new blog post is published, the title of the new post will automatically appear in the homepage and the oldest will be removed.

Luckily, site designers do not need complex programming skills to manipulate RSS. There are several sites that make incorporating RSS relatively painless. Feedwind and RSSInclude are two examples where designers can sign up for free and create a box that reads RSS feeds and displays them on a site. A designer just needs to know how to cut and paste the link to the RSS feed. The services provide code that can then be pasted into a webpage.

Designers can also use RSS to send content to social media sites. Twitterfeed is an example of a service that takes an RSS feed and turns each new post into a tweet with a link back to the original source. A library's blog RSS feed can be easily fed into a Twitter account so that community members can follow the Twitter stream and open posts that are of interest. Additionally, followers can retweet posts and reply to them. Similarly, a tool like RSS Graffiti can be used to incorporate RSS feeds into a Facebook account. RSS Graffiti is a Facebook app where multiple RSS feeds can be pulled into a Facebook page. When an RSS feed is updated, the content automatically updates on Facebook. An additional tool that may be useful for library site designers is an aggregator like Yahoo! Pipes, which can be used to pull together multiple RSS feeds into a single RSS feed. This new feed can be incorporated into social media sites so that updates from multiple blogs can be aggregated into a single account.

At the end of Chapter 4, I discussed the flexibility of blogs. Blogs remain the backbone of content distribution via social media because of the flexibility of RSS feeds. With a little setup time, a library's blog can become the source of content across multiple social media sites. A blog can feed content into a library's homepage, Twitter account, Facebook and other sources. Community members can connect with the library in the avenue that is most convenient for them. Posts from library social media tools will flow to users and be incorporated into their daily information consumption. For library staff members, the use of RSS can add a great deal of efficiency to social media use. Instead of having one person managing the Twitter account, another managing Facebook and another updating the library's blog, one person can post to the blog and all of the other accounts will be updated. This is especially useful for smaller libraries where staffing may not permit one person for each social media tool. One person can update multiple social media tools with a single blog post.

Learning how to utilize RSS may seem overwhelming at first, but cheap help is available online. YouTube has many short videos that help explain the how to incorporate this into HTML sites. Videos on Twitterfeed and RSS Graffiti are also available on YouTube. The abilities to search on YouTube and copy code are the most important skills in pulling RSS into websites and social media tools. Getting feeds to function properly may take a bit of playing around and testing, but librarians with basic knowledge of web design can make RSS into an effective tool.

OPACs, subscription tools and social media

Social media tools are connecting tools. They provide a social context around content. This is a powerful idea for libraries and librarians. The online revolution has seen card catalogs transform into online public access catalogs (OPACs), paper indices transform into subscription databases, and physical formats migrate online. The next phase for library research tools is to take the online search tools and fully integrate them with the web's social layer. This transformation is well underway.

Many integrated library systems are allowing users to incorporate functionality into social media sites. For instance, several ILS vendors are making OPAC interfaces in Facebook so that users can search collections in Facebook. Email alerts about overdue items are standard in most ILS installations. Messages in Facebook or Twitter are a logical next step. News sites such as the Huffington Post allow users to log into the site with their Facebook accounts, and it is no stretch to imagine library systems working with Facebook to make this functionality available. The incorporation of "Share on Facebook" or "Tweet this" buttons in OPAC results seems to make sense.

Book reviews, tags and comments are a regular part of online life within library information tools. The integration of a library ILS with social media will be commonplace within a very short amount of time. Connecting with subscription databases and online journals will be equally as common. These connections can enable easy sharing of library content. Social media will not be just an extra, fringe service, but a more integrated part of a library's operations.

The death of social media pages

Social media are becoming increasingly vital in supporting library services as communication tools, information-sharing platforms, and a social layer for library research tools. Even as these tools become more prevalent, managers and leaders must remember that the social media phenomenon is still relatively new. Serious tests of business models and organizational systems will come down the road, and some social media tools are bound to die away. Additionally, library leaders may start a social media page for a library, but users may not follow. Sometimes staff energy is better used in other directions, so managers may decide to stop using a particular site. Letting a page die can be very difficult especially if there are a few active users. Abandoning users can be painful, but sometimes it might be necessary. The question for managers is how we let these sites die.

Managers should not be afraid to pull the plug if sites are not being used. Time is a precious commodity so most libraries cannot afford to waste staff time on services that are not utilized. Of course, managers should take care not to pull the plug too early, because it takes time to attract users and build an active online presence.

Ideally, when social media services are abandoned, users should be given alternatives in service. For instance, when libraries pulled the plug on MySpace pages, many of them could redirect users to Facebook or blogs as an alternative. If nothing else, users should be directed back to the library's homepage. Once a library has made a connection with users, care should be taken to keep that connection in place. Therefore, users should be given a warning about the end of a library's social media site as early as possible, and they should be given an explanation so that they understand the reasoning behind the decision. Some users will be particularly fond of a site, and they may be frustrated or even angry when a service is discontinued. Explanations may not eliminate all frustration, but they may help.

Importantly, social media sites that are abandoned should be locked down as much as possible. For instance, if a blog is no longer being updated, a link back to the library's homepage should be provided and all comments should be turned off. If possible, the blog should automatically redirect users back to the library's main site. Problems may arise from abandoned sites where visitors can still post comments. Abandoned sites will attract comment spam like circling vultures. Managers, directors and governing boards will not want a library's name associated with adult sites, poker sites and the other usual spam suspects.

Unified voices

The library's homepage should bring together all of the online services, tools and informational pages into a somewhat coherent system. As loosely-coupled systems, libraries require an overarching design that connects the various areas of service and the diverse ways that these areas of service may connect to segments of the community. Connecting the different voices within the organization requires vision and leadership.

7

Leadership: big ideas do not have to be that big

Abstract: Social media tools can be leadership tools. By advancing topics of interest to the local community, offering support for local initiatives, and promoting library services to better the community, library staff members can extend themselves into the lives and activities of their users. Kouzes and Posner (2007) describe the practices of successful leaders: model the way, inspire a shared vision, challenge the process, enable others to act, and encourage the heart—practices which can also be applied to social media. These tools can play a role in transforming librarianship itself to answer R. David Lankes' call for "new librarianship." Libraries are not about collections or buildings but about creating knowledge in communities. Leaders and managers can build a curriculum for a library that targets learning goals based on community needs. Leaders must anticipate needs, but they should not fool themselves into thinking they can see the future. Major changes are unpredictable. The change from physically stored information to a digitally dominant information ecosystem clearly demonstrates the diversity of information needs in society. Libraries have an opportunity to redefine themselves within this diversity.

Key words: social media, Facebook, leadership, future of libraries, ebooks, new librarianship

Introduction

Food has become an important issue on our campus recently. We have students who struggle to pay for rent, transportation and food before considering paying for textbooks, school supplies, fees and tuition. Our college's charitable foundation has emergency scholarships to help students out of tight spots. For these reasons, faculty and staff have started to talk about food and nutrition for students as a matter of supporting them in their education.

For many years, our faculty has held an annual food drive and our library has held an annual "food for fines" program where patrons can donate food in place of paying an overdue fine, but several faculty members have started to discuss taking these initiatives a step further by creating a food pantry on our campus to support students. These faculty members told me about a service learning class project they were developing which focused on food services and food pantries. I thought these were great projects and that the library should offer support.

I asked one of our librarians to write some posts to one of our blogs. She did great work writing about food pantries on other campuses, food and sustainability, urban agriculture and volunteer organizations in our community that focus on food. These posts were thoughtful and well researched. We sent them to the faculty, and they, in turn, shared them with students. These posts did not invent a food pantry or cause one to appear magically on campus; neither did they feed hungry students. Nevertheless, these posts did achieve some important things. First, they offered important moral support to faculty members and students who were trying to move a big project forward. Second, they offered ideas and information as context around the topic. Finally, they linked to resources within the library's collections, on the web, and in the community.

Connecting with our community didn't take monumental resources or effort. After a semester of planning, the faculty member who initially discussed the food pantry idea announced that they would indeed open a food pantry on campus and that they were initiating a large food drive. The librarian who posted about food was a voice offering support and ideas. We plan to continue.

Through efforts like this, I want our librarians to be leaders in advancing ideas on campus. Our library should be the intellectual hub of the campus. We should be the place where ideas blossom, whether the ideas are online or in our physical space. My library's blogs are not writing tools or social media tools; rather, they are *leadership tools*. They are places where we capture ideas and make them shareable. When our librarian wrote about food, we didn't just hope that these blog posts would serendipitously find their way to the right people. We purposefully emailed them to the right people. We told this faculty member and their students that we had written these posts for them and that we hoped that their project would succeed. Of course, the fact that other people around the world can find these blog posts is a fringe benefit for us. In fact, through Twitter we have seen our posts shared by local food activists.

If social media are to be leadership tools, then librarians need to frame them around leadership. Leadership gurus Kouzes and Posner (2007) define five practices of leaders. Managers and leaders must keep these practices in mind as they give their staff and community a voice around social media:

- *Model the way*: Planners and technologists often assume they can implement a technology and then they get out of the way. This might work when the uses of technology are obvious, but it will never work when the vision for the technology is novel and beyond the common assumptions. It also means that *telling* them about new approaches to the technology will not be anywhere near as effective as *showing* them how to do it.

- *Inspire a shared vision*: The emphasis here is on the word *shared*. As discussed in Chapter 4, finding a focus around social media tools should be a group activity. Together, staff members can build a vision for what social media tools can accomplish, but it takes leadership to keep that vision alive. Fear of risk will keep staff happily within routine, so leaders must keep the vision front and center in order to drive change.

- *Challenge the process*: In loosely-coupled systems, the disconnect between inputs (time and resources) and outputs (services to the community) can allow habit to trump continuous improvement. It is easy to fall into the we've-always-done-it-this-way trap. As discussed in Chapter 3, social media can drive change by enabling information sharing across the organization. Leaders know this and work to encourage open sharing.

- *Enable others to act*: Social media cannot function as a one-person show. If they are to be truly effective, everyone must play along. This means leaders must help people grow their skills even if they are just starting out. This may mean that some people will need a great deal of support. Each blog post may take handholding and patience. However, leaders must remain committed to the idea that all staff should access and contribute to social media tools.

- *Encourage the heart*: Leaders take time to recognize good work and celebrate the successes of employees. For social media, this is important because celebrating good work with social media also celebrates social media's connection to the organization's goals. Recognizing innovative or thoughtful uses of social media encourages future utilization of these tools.

When it comes to managing social media, leadership is essential. I started this book with the notion that managing social media does not revolve around technological questions. The challenges in managing social media come from human challenges such as defining responsibilities, organizing workflows, establishing goals and creating a shared vision. All of these challenges hinge on leadership.

New librarianship

I also started this book with the two questions that I believe organizations must address in using social media: *how will a particular tool be useful* and *what information will the organization choose to share?* Answering these questions requires an understanding of an organization's goals and community. Answering them effectively as a functional organization requires structure built around coordination tools and systems that enhance the loosely-coupled nature of libraries. Social media enable librarians to capture the knowledge created everyday within the community, and to play an integral role in information distribution and creation within the community. However, librarians face a challenge to be more than just distribution networks.

In his groundbreaking book, *The Atlas of New Librarianship*, R. David Lankes challenges us to rethink our view of libraries and librarians:

> Libraries are not caretakers of artifacts. Librarians are not finders of things. Librarians are much more profoundly useful and powerful. Librarians are in the

knowledge business. They—you—facilitate the creation of knowledge, and by doing so you improve society. Rather than building book museums, we—you and I—must build edifices of bricks and code to promote knowledge. Where once Carnegie built temples to books, we shall build workshops of the mind. (Lankes, 2011: 63)

Lankes presents a vision for librarians to build upon what we have been and engage our communities to become something new. Lankes outlines how librarians facilitate knowledge creation. He defines four pieces:

- *Access*: It brings together conversants and appropriate resources to build knowledge.

- *Knowledge*: Through a curriculum, it helps novices quickly gain the requisite knowledge to participate in conversations.

- *Environment*: Through community-based governance systems, it ensures a feeling of ownership and trust with the community.

- *Motivation*: It allows interested community members to follow their intrinsic interests, as well as create publication systems based on the community's norms of recognition. (Lankes, 2011: 101)

These four pieces interact to create a people-powered, people-focused, physical and virtual organization that generates knowledge through community conversation and interaction. I am especially intrigued by Lankes' idea of a *curriculum* for a library, which he sees as the learning needs of the community. Librarians enact their curriculum by putting services in place to meet these needs. Librarians already do this to some degree, but Lankes' discussion suggests making learning goals more apparent and better defined. Some academic and school libraries have done this around information literacy and the formal school curriculum. But Lankes is suggesting something beyond this traditional approach within education. He is suggesting that librarians in all types of libraries move beyond simply organizing and acquiring resources so that other people can create knowledge. He is suggesting that libraries create a plan that ties together resources, events, space, workshops and other services aimed at learning. This is a more targeted and richer approach than simply thinking about service populations. This is thinking about the goals held by members of these populations.

Lankes' visionary definition of "new librarianship" puts the librarian at the center of libraries. It is not about collections, buildings or online tools. It is about what librarians do—and librarians do many things. While not all of their jobs require social media, it is clear that social media have an important role to play in Lankes' vision. Social media represent not only a way to connect, but a way to enact the library's curriculum. Social media tools can become learning environments that build knowledge, enable idea sharing and allow community members to advance their goals. Thus, when librarians ask themselves *what information will the organization choose to share with social media*, they should consider how this information advances knowledge creation and their curricular goals.

No one can predict the future

Leaders must work with staff to create a vision for the future, but they should never go so far as to believe that they can predict the future. When managers get overconfident and lock themselves into a particular vision of what is coming down the road, they limit their ability to react to new changes. This is why Lankes' emphasis on *librarians* over *libraries* is important. People can shift and change to meet evolving needs. Collections, buildings and online resources do not really do much without people. They surely do not change.

Leaders know that the next big social media application is just over the horizon. Facebook, Twitter and Pinterest may be hot now, but they could be yesterday's news overnight. When managers and leaders think about social media, they should think about people. They should consider ways that staff members come together to enable knowledge creation in their community. Managing social media is about managing the structures, connections and workflows between people (Figure 7.1).

Prognosticators abound within librarianship and the blogosphere. They offer advice and direction about the

Figure 7.1 The Undergrad Library at the University of Illinois at Urbana Champaign engages students through Twitter

unfolding impact of technology on what we do. But as Nassim Taleb outlines in *The Black Swan*, prediction carries an inherent problem:

> Prediction requires knowing about technologies that will be discovered in the future. But that very knowledge would almost automatically allow us to start developing those technologies right away. Ergo, we do not know what we will know. (Taleb, 2007: 173)

If librarians could have recognized the impact of Google, then librarians would have invented it. When Google was being invented, librarians were busily indexing the internet by hand and talking about the poor search results on Alta Vista. After Google arrived, searching for information was never the same.

Predicting the future

When people hear the word "library," they think of books (De Rosa et al., 2011). There is no way around the fact that the library brand remains closely tied to books. Unfortunately, it doesn't take a clairvoyant to know that times are changing quickly. Books are not what they used to be. As a profession, librarians offer so many valuable skills beyond just delivering books, and many librarians are working to break out of traditional stereotypes. In some ways, I am trying to do this with this book. But, regardless of these efforts, the future of libraries and librarians is still tied to books, at least for the short term. The ways that books evolve will influence the ways that libraries evolve. Libraries and publishers are feeling the shockwaves caused by the move from physical books to ebooks. Much has been and will continue to be written on this shift. I do not intend to offer a comprehensive view of this change. Nevertheless, some changes are noteworthy in the context of social media and libraries.

One of the important lessons of the digital shift is that books were used in the past to store information because books were all that society had. Many texts function better in an alternative format. The reality that the *Encyclopaedia Britannica* is no longer available in print is a testament to this (BBC News, 2012). Next to the digital format, the printed encyclopedia makes little sense. The only value of alphabetizing entries is in terms of searching. The "A" volume communicates where a particular entry will be found. Locating "alligator" in the same text as "Azerbaijan" offers no value to the content of the text. The encyclopedia functions much better online where entries can be linked together, organized into larger categories and searched more easily.

Just as the encyclopedia makes no sense as a book, so there are other types of traditionally book-based content, texts and information tools that can break out of the medium. Innovations editor for *Futurist* magazine, Thomas Fry (2012), offers the following list of media replacing books:

- games;
- digital books;
- audio books;
- newspapers;
- magazines;
- music;
- [online] photos;
- videos;
- television;
- [online] movies;

- [satellite and internet] radio;
- blogs;
- podcasts;
- apps;
- [online] presentations;
- courseware;
- [online] personal networks.

Fry's goal here is to demonstrate the diversification of information options before us. Some of the forms on this list have been around for a long time, and at first glance, it may not be clear how they may be replacing books. For instance, "music" has been around for quite a long time. How can it be replacing books? The big change around music has been the ease of listening. Throughout the twentieth century, access to music and ease of listening improved from phonographs, to LPs, to cassette tapes, and to CDs. Now, the shift to online has made it possible to carry hours and hours of music and to incorporate music into home entertainment systems and automobiles. Now that music can be transported and accessed so easily it is encroaching into leisure time that was once dedicated to reading. Many of the above examples represent a battle for time that for decades had been dominated by books. The ease of access associated with the online world has made it much easier to exchange ideas. All of these cut into roles that books played in the past.

For instance in 2011, economist Tyler Cowen chose to forgo the traditional publishing route for his book, *The Great Stagnation*, instead releasing it as a 15 000-word ebook that can be downloaded as a PDF. Noting that his book is similar in length to the economics pamphlets published in the seventeenth century, Cowen claimed to be aiming for those readers whom he terms "infovores," that is, individuals that absorb a great deal of content outside of the general reading public (Leonhardt, 2011). *The Great Stagnation* represents a diversity in publishing that has only recently become possible.

This diversity is removing barriers to access for information distribution. In the past, only a few people were able to publish information. Books, magazines, newspapers, music and film required a great deal of training, the ability to manage large organizations, a touch of luck, and the ability to create a profitable product to get information to the public in a significant way. Small-scale newsletters and self-published books existed, but had marginal impact and held a negative connotation. The digital shift is opening up access to the publication of all types of media as never before. Thanks to social media, self-publication has become the standard. The book publishing industry has realized that self-publication is a great way to discover new writers. Today, the nice neat information world of the past is a memory. In some ways, it was never nice and neat, but digital information has messed it all up forever more. Everyone can publish, create videos, write music and blog.

Identity crisis

In the past, libraries dealt in books because that was the primary means of sharing information. Now, libraries face an identity crisis. Librarians and regular library users know that library services are much broader than just books. As loosely-coupled systems, libraries have the potential to adapt to community needs. Structurally, libraries can grow and morph. They can create and share innovations across the organization. Their primary limitation is the creativity of their people. The ways that libraries answer the question facing them about identity will be up to the people who work within them and how they engage with their communities in knowledge creation.

This book is my argument for social media's role in that redefinition. Social media represent not only a tool for communication, but also a tool for knowledge creation and learning. Social media can also be a tool for leadership. Libraries have experimented with social media tools. Increasingly, they understand the technology, but how have they connected the tools with their core missions?

As library leaders and managers work within their organizations to create a new vision for the future, they should remember these two pieces of advice from Kouzas and Posner:

- "You can't believe in the messenger if you don't know what the messenger believes."
- "You can't be the messenger until you're clear about what you believe." (Kouzas and Posner, 2007: 47)

The library's mission as knowledge creation centers for their communities must remain at the center of what they do. This is the vision that helps library staff to make sense of their work. This is what provides purpose and understanding around these tools.

Glossary

I offer this glossary as a clarification for how I am using specific terms and jargon. These definitions are not intended to be perfect or make a scholarly statement. I hope that this list will be a quick reference for those who are new to social media. Readers who are interested in longer treatments of these terms may wish to check Wikipedia, where they will find fairly reasonable definitions.

Audacity: A free digital audio editing program.

Blog: A website typically of short articles (100–500 words) updated regularly and organized by date with the newest posts at the top of the page. Blogs are often thought of as online journals, but have evolved into more news-like sites covering a specific topic or related topics. Blogs have one or multiple authors contributing posts.

Blogger: A free blog platform owned by Google.

Facebook: One of the largest social networking sites.

Google⁺: A social networking site launched by Google.

Google Groups: Online discussion groups owned by Google that often include discussion boards, areas to share files and group email lists. Google Groups are free and can be made private.

Delicious: A social bookmarking site used for saving and organizing links.

Digg: A social news site where users can "digg" an article giving it an online vote used to rank it against other articles. Websites can embed a Digg button so that readers can easily "digg" an article thus helping to increase its exposure. Users can use the ratings to discover articles.

Feed: A general term used to describe a regularly updated flow of content (articles, images, video, etc.) often used for specific technologies as in Twitter feed, news feed, or RSS feed.

Flickr: A free image-sharing site where users can upload and tag images. These images can be shared via feed into other sites or social media services.

FourSquare: A location-based social media site where users "check-in" to restaurants, bars and other places as a way to connect with friends.

Hashtags: Words or phrases used in social media sites (primarily Twitter) that act as makeshift subject headings which tie together posts by users who are writing on similar topics.

Hootsuite: Software for managing social media sites. Hootsuite allows users to post to multiple Facebook accounts, Twitter accounts and other social media sites.

HSX: The Hollywood Stock Exchange is a trading market for stocks based on the earnings of Hollywood films.

HTML: Hypertext Markup Language is the primary language used to create webpages.

InTrade: An online futures market where users buy options on questions about world events.

LinkedIn: A social media site used primarily for business and professional contacts.

Microblog: A social media site where the size of posts is limited to encourage regular postings and fast browsing. Twitter is often classified as a microblog.

MP3: A common audio file-type used most often for downloading music or podcasts.

MySpace: One of the first social media sites to reach widespread popularity. With the rise of Facebook, MySpace became less dominant.

Ning: A social networking and discussion group site where users can organize their own groups around topics or interests. These groups can be public or private.

PDF: A standard file-type for documents.

Pinterest: A social networking and photo sharing site based on the concept of a virtual pin-board, where users "pin" images and visual links to websites. Information is shared in theme-based clusters.

Photo sharing sites: Websites where users upload and distribute digital images which are often tagged based on subject or content. Flickr is one of the most popular examples of photo-sharing sites.

Podcast: An online audio cast that utilizes MP3 files and XML. Podcasts are often associated with Apple's iPod and iTunes, but are actually available on any device or software able to play MP3s. Generally, podcasts are semi-regular audio segments resembling radio broadcasts.

Reddit: A social news site where users submit and vote on news stories.

RSS: A standardized file-type that includes labeled content which can be incorporated into other sites. An RSS "feed" is a stream of content from a social media site such as a blog or podcast.

Scribd: A social media site used to share documents of various types.

Slideshare: A social media site used for sharing presentation slides.

Snopes: A US-based website that debunks or confirms rumors and myths.

Social bookmarking: Social media sites that store and organize links to online resources. Delicious is one of the more popular examples of social bookmarking sites.

Social media: Online services that enable two-way sharing and communication between users, organizations and larger communities. Social media are often recognized as a key component of Web 2.0, which is an effort to differentiate from the static web of the late 1990s.

Social networking: Any online service that allows users to connect socially sharing updates, photos, links and other social connections. Facebook, LinkedIn and Google+ are the most well-known social networking sites.

Stumbledupon: Social media site where user ratings and preferences enable the discovery of new sites and resources.

Tags: Descriptive keywords assigned to websites, images and other files.

Tumblr: A microblogging site often used to post media.

Tweetup: A meetup of people who tweet around a topic.

Twitter: A microblogging site utilizing text of 140 characters or less.

Web 2.0: Term used to describe a wide range of web-based tools and services that are more interactive and user-driven than the more static, page-driven websites that came to prominence during the initial growth of the web. The term "Web 2.0" has become somewhat passé in some circles.

Wiki: A type of social media site where pages can be easily edited and updated.

Wikipedia: User-created and organized encyclopedia.

Wordpress: A free blogging platform.

XML: A standard file-type where content is "marked-up" or described for purposes of display within websites. XML is often utilized by social media sites.

Yahoo! Groups: Online discussion groups owned by Yahoo! that are free and open any users. Groups can be made private.

YouTube: A social media site where users share online videos.

Bibliography

Anderson, C. (2009) *Free: The Future of a Radical Price.* New York: Hyperion.

Anderson, K. (2011) "The protestor." *Time.* Available at: *http://www.time.com/time/person-of-the-year/2011/* (accessed June 18, 2012).

BBC News (2004) "'Blog' picked as word of the year." Available at: *http://news.bbc.co.uk/2/hi/technology/4059291.stm* (accessed June 6, 2008).

BBC News (2012) "Encyclopaedia Britannica ends its famous print edition." Available at: *http://www.bbc.co.uk/news/business-17362698* (accessed June 18, 2012).

Blood, R. (2002) *The Weblog Handbook: Practical Advice on Creating and Maintaining your Blog.* Cambridge, MA: Perseus Pubications.

Carr, D. (2012) "Twitter is all in good fun, until it isn't." *New York Times*, 13 February. p. B1.

De Rosa. C., Cantrell, J., Carslon, M., Gallagher, M., Hawk, J., Sturtz, C., Gauder, B., Cellentani, D., Dalrymple, T. and Olszewski, L. (2011) *Perceptions of Libraries, 2010: Context and Community.* Dublin, OH: OCLC.

Dumitru, B. (2009) "The risks of social networking and the corporate network." Available at: *http://www.itbusinessedge.com/cm/community/features/guestopinions/blog/the-risks-of-social-networking-and-the-corporate-network/?cs=33877* (accessed June 18, 2012).

Fry, T. (2012) "17 Forms replacing books." Available at: *http://www.futuristspeaker.com/2012/03/future-libraries-and-the-17-forms-of-information-replacing-books/* (accessed June 18, 2012).

Gerolimos, M. (2011) "Academic libraries on Facebook: An analysis of users' comments." *D-Lib Magazine* 17(11/12), Available at: *http://www.dlib.org/dlib/november11/gerolimos/11gerolimos.html* (accessed June 18, 2012).

Gleick, J. (2011) *The Information: A History, a Theory, a Flood*. New York: Pantheon Books.

Grossman, L. (2006) "You—yes, you—are Time's person of the year." *Time*. Available at: *http://www.time.com/time/magazine/article/0,9171,1570810,00.html* (accessed June 18, 2012).

Hachten, W., and Scotton, J. (2012) *The World News Prism: Challenges of Digital Communication*. Chichester: Wiley-Blackwell.

Hampton, K., Sessions Goulet, L., Marlos, C. and Rainie, L. (2012) "Why most Facebook users get more than they give." *Pew Internet and American Life Project*. Available at: *http://www.pewinternet.org/Reports/2012/Facebook-users.aspx* (accessed June 18, 2012).

Hilbert, M. and López, P. (2011) "The world's technological capacity to store, communicate, and compute information." *Science* 332(6025): 60–5.

Hughes, A. (1998) *The Causes of the English Civil War*. Basingstoke: Palgrave.

Jefferson, T., Gilreath, J. and Wilson, D. L. (1989) *Thomas Jefferson's Library: A Catalog with the Entries in his Own Order*. Washington, DC: Library of Congress.

Kouzes, J. M. and Posner, B. Z. (2007) *The Leadership Challenge* (4th edn). San Francisco, CA: Jossey-Bass.

Lankes, R. D. (2011) *The Atlas of New Librarianship*. Cambridge, MA: MIT Press.

Lefebvre, R. C. (2007) "The new technology: The consumer as participant rather than target audience." *Social Marketing Quarterly* 13: 31–42.

Leonhardt, D. (2011) "A conversation with Tyler Cowen." *New York Times' Economix blog: Explaining the Science of Everyday Life.* Available at: *http://economix.blogs. nytimes.com/2011/02/03/a-conversation-with-tyler-cowen/* (accessed June 18, 2012).

Lessig, L. (1999) *Code and Other Laws of Cyberspace.* New York: Basic Books.

Levine, R. (2011) *Free Ride: How Digital Parasites Are Destroying the Culture Business, and How the Culture Business Can Fight Back.* New York: Doubleday.

Miller, M. (2010) "East Stroudsburg U. suspends professor for Facebook posts." *Chronicle of Higher Education Wired campus.* Available at: *http://chronicle.com/blogs/ wiredcampus/east-stroudsburg-u-suspends-professor-for-ffacebook-posts/21498* (accessed June 18, 2012).

Moynihan, C. (2012) "Occupy Wall Street claims the city ruined its library." *New York Times.* Available at: *http:// cityroom.blogs.nytimes.com/2012/02/09/occupy-wall-street-charges-city-ruined-its-library/* (accessed June 18, 2012).

Naisbitt, J. (1982) *Megatrends: Ten New Directions Transforming our Lives.* New York: Warner Books.

Nielsen, J. (2000) "Why you only need to test with 5 users," *Jakob Nielson's Alertbox.* Available at: *http://www.useit. com/alertbox/20000319.html* (accessed June 18, 2012).

Nielsen, J. (2003) "Usability 101: Introduction to usability," *Jakob Nielson's Alertbox.* Available at: *http://www.useit. com/alertbox/20030825.html* (accessed June 18, 2012).

Parr, B. (2009) "Facebook chat: 1 billion messages sent per day." Available at: *http://mashable.com/2009/06/15/ fbchat-facebook-billion/* (accessed June 18, 2012).

Pasetsky, M. (2011) "Osama Bin Laden is dead: News explodes on Twitter." *Forbes*. Available at: *http://www.forbes.com/ sites/markpasetsky/2011/05/01/osama-bin-laden-is-dead-news-explodes-on-twitter/* (accessed June 18, 2012).

Plunkett, J. (2012) "Don't break stories on Twitter, BBC journalists told." Available at: *http://www.guardian.co. uk/media/2012/feb/08/twitter-bbc-journalists* (accessed June 18, 2012).

Rogers, E. (1995) *Diffusion of Innovations* (4th edn). New York: The Free Press.

Rosenthal, E. (2011) "Reinventing post offices in a digital world." *New York Times*. Available at: *http://www. nytimes.com/2011/10/31/world/europe/deutsche-post-reinvents-services-in-a-digital-world.html* (accessed June 18, 2012).

Sharpe, K. (2000) *Reading Revolutions: The Politics of Reading in Early Modern England*. New Haven, CT: Yale.

Shirky, C. (2005) "Clay Shirky on institutions vs. collaboration." Available at: *http://www.ted.com/talks/ clay_shirky_on_institutions_versus_collaboration.html*.

Sky News (2009) "Sacked for calling job boring on Facebook." Available at: *http://news.sky.com/home/uk-news/article/15230508* (accessed June 18, 2012).

Smith, A. (2011) "Why Americans use social media." *Pew Internet and American Life Project*. Available at: *http:// www.pewinternet.org/Reports/2011/Why-Americans-Use-Social-Media.aspx* (accessed June 18, 2012).

Surowiecki, J. (2004) *The Wisdom of Crowds: Why the Many Are Smarter than the Few and How Collective Wisdom Shapes Business, Economies, Societies, and Nations*. New York: Doubleday.

Surowiecki, J. (2010) "The next level." *New Yorker* 86(32): 28.

Taleb, N. (2007) *The Black Swan: The Impact of the Highly Improbable*. New York: Random House.

Velez, J. (2011) "An unusual library finds a new home." *New York Times*. Available at: *http://www.nytimes.com/2011/11/13/us/an-unusual-library-finds-a-new-home.html?_r=1* (accessed June 18, 2012).

Waghorn, D. (2010) "Soldier's Facebook post scuppers army raid." Available at: *http://news.sky.com/home/article/15567680* (accessed June 18, 2012).

Weick, K. (1974) "Middle range theories of social systems." *Behavioral Science* 19: 357–67.

Weick, K. (1976) "Educational organizations as loosely coupled systems." *Administrative Science Quarterly*. 21(1): 1–19.

Weick, K. (1982) "Administering education in loosely coupled schools." *Phi Delta Kappan* 63: 673–76.

Weinberger, D. (2007) *Everything is Miscellaneous: The Power of the New Digital Disorder*. New York: Times Books.

Weinberger, D. (2012) *Too Big to Know: Rethinking Knowledge Now that the Facts Aren't the Facts, Experts are Everywhere, and the Smartest Person in the Room is the Room*. New York: Basic Books.

Williment, K., Jones-Grant, T., Sommers, D. (2011). From Project to Branch Integration and Sustainability: Community-Led Work at Halifax Public Library. *Public Libraries Online*. Available at: *http://www.publiclibraries online.org/magazines/featured-articles/project-branch-integration-and-sustainability-community-led-work-halifax* (accessed June 18, 2012).

World Bank (2010) "Internet users" (data file). Available at: *http://data.worldbank.org/indicator/IT.NET.USER.P2* (accessed June 18, 2012).

Index

CPSIA information can be obtained at www.ICGtesting.com
Printed in the USA
BVOW03s0857011013

332588BV00005B/248/P